The Story of

P&O

THE PENINSULAR AND ORIENTAL

STEAM NAVIGATION

COMPANY

'Victoria, by the Grace of God . . .'
The Royal Charter of Incorporation of
The Peninsular and Oriental Steam Navigation Company,
dated 31 December 1840.

The Story of

P&O

THE PENINSULAR AND ORIENTAL STEAM NAVIGATION COMPANY

David Howarth and Stephen Howarth

WEIDENFELD AND NICOLSON
LONDON

ENDPAPERS

(*Front*)
Detail from 'The *William Fawcett* and HMS *Queen*, 1837'.
(Watercolour by Frank Murray, 1893)

(*Back*)
Detail from 'The Hulk of HMS *Queen*
towing past P&O SS *Valetta*, 1889'.
(Watercolour by Frank Murray, 1893)

Published in Great Britain by
George Weidenfeld & Nicolson Limited
91 Clapham High Street
London SW4 7TA

ISBN 0 297 78965 1

Printed in Italy

Contents

The Arms granted to P&O
on 16 June in its Centenary year, 1937.

Foreword

Sir Jeffrey Sterling cbe
Chairman
The Peninsular and Oriental Steam Navigation Company

The one hundred and fifty years of The Peninsular & Oriental Steam Navigation Company is much more than the story of a great commercial enterprise. It is the very stuff of history. David Howarth and Stephen Howarth have in my view told the tale with skill and perception plotting the company's course through the great tides of the 19th & 20th centuries from its origins as a single office in the City of London running a handful of small paddle steamers.

P&O has had moments of greatness and high drama, of disaster and near extinction – its history has never been dull. Above all it is a record of human endeavour and achievement, and in commending it to you I salute the thousands of men and women who preceded us, in peace and war, throughout a century and a half, who made this book possible.

I

STEAM AND SAIL

P&O is as old as seagoing steamships: 1837 is accepted as the year of its birth.

That was a most exciting time, the time when the 'dark satanic mills' of the industrial revolution invaded and overwhelmed the foreshore of great estuaries, the Thames, the Clyde, the Mersey and the Avon. The homely sounds of saws, planes, chisels and adzes vanished from yards where the ancient crafts of shipbuilding had been pursued for centuries, and with them went the sweet scent of wood freshly cut. Each forward-looking yard had to have a foundry in it or near it, where the huge cylinders and pistons of steam engines were cast, some of them 7 feet in diameter and 6 feet in stroke, and rolling mills where the plates of iron boilers were shaped and rivetted. And within a few years, the raucous sounds and hot smells of ironworking had spread to the hulls themselves when the pioneers began to think about iron ships.

It was a time of intense competition between rival shipbuilders, engine-builders, captains, ports and routes, a time when records were only made to be broken. There was ferocious rivalry too between entrepreneurs, the business men behind the shipbuilding. It is hard to say why so many rich men were tempted to own a steamship, or a fleet of them. Perhaps it had more air of adventure than owning, say, a cotton mill. Perhaps they even imagined themselves on the bridge giving orders, or taking the wheel and steering their ship to faraway seas without the carefully guarded skills of old-fashioned sailors. But it was a very risky investment and a quite remarkable proportion of them went bankrupt. Those whose sights were set on the longest voyages were naturally divided by geography, some looking to the westward routes out of England and some to the east. The most famous and successful of those who headed west was Samuel Cunard, and of those who went east P&O. Both of them are still flourishing now, 150 years later.

It is true that a few steamships had been launched and completed before P&O existed, and some of them had sometimes gone to sea. But all, for the next 30 years, carried a full suit of sails which they used to save fuel when the wind was fair, and also to keep the ship under way when the engines broke down, as they often did. So there was always a question, when is a steamship not a steamship, and some of the early claims for steam were somewhat bogus. The American ship *Savannah*, for example, claimed to be the first steamship to cross the Atlantic in 1819. But she was built as a sailing ship and had only a small auxiliary engine with detachable paddle wheels which could be taken off and stowed on deck; and stowed on deck they were for all except eight hours of the 21-day crossing. A much longer voyage was made by the steamship *Enterprize* from London to Calcutta in 1821. It was over

(*Opposite above*)
Before steamers were perfected, world maritime trade relied on sailing ships: cheap and easy to run, but totally reliant on weather and tides, unable to operate a regular service. Even the East India Company's fast packet *Swallow*, built in 1777, was at the mercy of the monsoon, and nothing much changed in the next sixty years.
(Oil by Thomas Luny, 1782)

(*Opposite below*)
General Steam Navigation Company's 56-ton *Eagle* packet passing Greenwich on her run from London to Margate in 1824. Successful early steamship companies such as GSN (acquired by P&O in 1920) concentrated on river, coastal or short cross-channel routes.
(Oil by Leslie Willcox, 1980)

9

Arthur Anderson
(1792–1868), the one-time
Shetland 'beach boy' who
became clerk and then
partner to London
shipbroker Brodie McGhie
Willcox, and like the older
man rose to become first a
Managing Director and then
Chairman of P&O, largely on
the basis of his imagination
and foresight.
(Oil by T. F. Dicksee, 1850)

11,000 miles and took 103 days, but she only started her engine on 64 of the days.

Several people were involved in the birth of P&O, but two men are regarded as its founders. Brodie McGhie Willcox and Arthur Anderson. In one way, they differed from most of the other would-be shipowners, for they were not rich men but were dragging themselves up out of poverty.

Very little is known about Willcox, except that he started as a shipbroker in 1815, 'with no influence and but limited pecuniary means', in an office at 46 Lime Street, a short walk from London Bridge. Anderson was a more colourful and adventurous person, likeable, kind and generous. He came from the Shetland Islands, and Shetlanders have often served with distinction in the Merchant Navy. His first job

Brodie McGhie Willcox
(1786–1862), whose business
acumen and experience
provided a perfect balance
for Anderson's flair in the
foundation and growth of
P&O.
(Oil by T.F.Dicksee, 1850)

was in curing fish, when he was 11. He narrowly escaped the press gang, but then volunteered for the Navy: it was and still is typical of a Shetlander to refuse to be told to do something, and then to do it of his own free will, and do it well. When Napoleon was exiled to Elba, Anderson's ship was paid off in Portsmouth; he walked to London because he had no money and lived there on the edge of starvation until he met Willcox, who gave him a job as a clerk. While he was still in his twenties, Willcox made him a partner, and in 1825 the two of them, trading as Willcox and Anderson, entered the perilous world of shipowning.

It is said, without much confirmation, that their first ship, and for quite a long time the only ship they owned, was a small American schooner which had gone ashore near Dover. They bought her where

In 1835 Willcox & Anderson chartered the 206-ton *William Fawcett*, built in 1828, to open their first, irregular 'Peninsular Steam' service to Spain and Portugal. Though she never ran on the mail contract service begun in 1837, she has traditionally been regarded as the first 'P&O' ship.
(Oil by S.D.Skillet, 1836)

she lay, salvaged her, fitted her out with some guns, and set her to work taking cargoes to Portugal; and on her first voyage, Anderson sailed with her.

In Portugal, he must certainly have met Mad Charlie. At the end of the wars many naval officers, ashore on half pay with no hope of another seagoing command, joined the navy of a foreign power, or better still went to a kingdom that had no navy and offered to found one. Mad Charlie (as the Navy called him) or rather Admiral Sir Charles Napier, was one of them. At the age of 64, under the pseudonym of Carlo de Fonza, he was founding a navy for the Queen of Portugal, who was fighting an insurrection. Anderson and his schooner were soon in the thick of gun-running for the Queen and her admiral, which no doubt was more exciting, more risky and more profitable, than carrying mundane cargoes. A little later, when the firm had chartered a very small steamer, Anderson had to take a pseudonym himself, for the whole thing was illegal. Calling himself Mr Smith, he brought two emissaries of the Queen to England disguised as his servants. They succeeded in their mission of raising money for the Queen's cause and luckily for everyone she won. Willcox and Anderson promptly began advertising voyages by steamship.

One of their first steamers was the *William Fawcett*, which is listed as the first in P&O's fleet, although her earliest voyages were made under charter. She was built in Liverpool in 1828: gross tonnage 206, horsepower 60, and Fawcett was the man who built her engine. Nobody at the time wrote anything of the discomfort of crossing the Bay of Biscay, notoriously stormy, in a paddle steamer of that size; they expected it but it must have been formidable. Any small ship is more sickening under power than under sail because sails steady her and give more rhythm to her motion. Paddles were never really suited to the open sea. When a paddle steamer pitched, both paddles came out of the water at once and let the engine race, then plunged in too deep and almost brought the engine to a stop. When she rolled, one paddle was too shallow and the other was too deep, and she proceeded like a corkscrew. Paddlers always rolled excessively because the paddle shaft had to be above the waterline and therefore the centre of gravity of the machinery was very high. Whatever happened, throughout it all was the slow endless thud of the engine, which in the early days had a single cylinder and ran at about 16 revolutions a minute: a thud every four seconds, and a rhythmic series of clanks and hisses between.

On returning from one of those adventures, one must imagine that Anderson met Willcox, who told him it was all very well, but they were losing money. Indeed, nobody trying to set up a regular long-distance steamship service anywhere had succeeded in making it pay. Even on the transatlantic run, where the capital investment was much bigger, bankruptcies were threatening. The Great Western Company itself, which had the advantage of the genius of Brunel the engineer as a ship designer, was heading for financial ruin. His first masterpiece the *Great Western* could easily reach New York but one steamer alone could not give a regular service; however good it was, it had to have time for refits and repairs, and while it was getting them the Great Western Company had nothing to put in its place. Willcox and Anderson were prepared to meet that difficulty by having a sufficient number of ships for the job.

It must have needed surprising self-confidence for two men without fame or fortune to stick to their ambition when so many richer and better known were failing. Willcox and Anderson knew exactly what they wanted to do and still believed they could do it. They wished to run a regular steamship service to Portugal and Spain, and issued a prospectus in 1834 giving the name of their proposed company: the Peninsular Steam Navigation Company. 'And Oriental' was added later, when they raised their sights to include the eastern Mediterranean. The Peninsular and Oriental Steam Navigation Company did sound rather cumbersome but abbreviated it yielded the memorable initials P&O, by which the company has been known ever since.

The earlier title began to be seen in advertisements in 1835, but for the next couple of years the service was far from regular. In 1837, however, the company advertised a fleet of seven steamships – and they were evidently real steamships – ships designed and built for engines with auxiliary sail, rather than ships like the *Savannah*, which were built for sail with auxiliary engines. All of them were said to be 'new, powerful, large and splendidly fitted up'. And two of them, the *Don*

P&O was seldom technologically venturesome. Not so Isambard Kingdom Brunel (1806–59), naval architect and civil engineer extraordinaire, seen here beside the launching chains of his gargantuan *Great Eastern* in 1858.

THE GREAT WESTERN STEAM SHIP CROSSING THE ATLANTIC.

Published by W. Everitt 1 Pulteney Bridge Both, & J. Mc Cormick, 45 Ludgate Hill, London

Even the genius of Brunel could not make a one-ship operation with no mail contract a paying proposition. P&O, always on the lookout for likely second-hand tonnage as its Eastern services developed, attempted unsuccessfully to buy the seven-year old *Great Western* in 1844.
(Lithograph by H. E. Hobson)

Juan and the *Tagus*, were claimed as the 'largest and most powerful that have yet been put afloat'. Perhaps they were but only for a very short time. The first of Brunel's three great steamers was 'put afloat' in Bristol in that same year and each of those in its turn was far bigger than any before it. But nobody then expected a superlative to last.

The reason why so many people were going broke was simple enough : steamships were extremely expensive both to build and to run. They were expensive to build because they needed sails, spars and rigging like any sailing ship, and the boilers, machinery and paddles were extra. They also needed full-sized sailing crews, plus crews of engineers. Above all, a sailing ship's power was free but a steamer had to have coal – and a great deal of coal because the early engines were extremely inefficient in terms of coal per mile.

There was another argument, beyond the frequent bankruptcies, against experiments with steam. Many expert and influential people still insisted that steamships would never succeed but would always be beaten by sail. Strangely, the leaders of the opposition to steam were the Lords of the Admiralty. All early steamships were driven by paddles and there were plausible arguments against having paddle wheels on a warship: they would be vulnerable to gun-fire and would get in the way of the ship's own broadsides. And, when the Navy won the sovereignty of the seas at the battle of Trafalgar it created for itself a worldwide responsibility to keep the peace at sea, and if it relied on steam, it would have to set up worldwide coaling stations and defend them. But the Navy also used a wholly illogical argument: it had a fleet of sailing ships far stronger than anyone else's, so why should it encourage new ideas that might make its own ships obsolete?

Yet they argued so fiercely that logic was lost to sight, and one is left to believe that prejudice was more important – that the Navy opposed steam simply because naval officers disliked it. In their view it was dirty and smelly. It covered their immaculate sails with smuts and their holystoned decks with coal dust. Above all, it was inartistic. There was skill and artistry in sailing a square-rigged ship, even in bringing her into harbour and laying her precisely alongside. In working a steam-engine there was none of that. Back in 1828, the First Lord had laid down the Navy's official opinion: 'Their Lordships feel it their bounden duty to discourage to the utmost of their ability the employ-ment of steam vessels, as they consider the introduction of steam is calculated to strike a fatal blow at the supremacy of the Empire.'

He had not troubled to support that opinion with logic and it would have been nearer the truth if he had made an exactly opposite statement. The British Empire was indeed at a moment of crisis, the same crisis that began the downfall of the Spanish Empire 250 years before. It had grown too big to be governed by laws and edicts distributed at the unpredictable speed of ships under sail. The key to its survival was the regularity of steam. Yet in this crisis the Royal Navy, the natural custodian of that key, refused to use it.

The Navy was the leading critic of steam but there were others. The most influential was not a seaman at all; he was the Rev. Dr Dionysius Lardner, an Irish cleric, Professor of Natural Philosophy and Astro-nomy at University College, London. At meetings in the early 1830s he proved by a totally false projection of statistics that no ship could steam for more than 15 days, or 2,080 miles, before it had burned all the coal it could carry; and therefore a voyage to New York was 'perfectly chimerical' and one might as well talk of a voyage to the moon. Another speaker in reply called him 'an impudent and ignorant empiric', for it was a subject that roused everyone's emotions. Soon after that public argument, an Atlantic crossing was almost commonplace and the doctor was discredited; but then he won another kind of fame by eloping with a lady called Mrs Heaviside, whose husband was a cavalry officer and successfully sued him for £8,000. He was forced to leave the country, crossed the Atlantic himself, made £40,000 on a lecture tour of the United States, and retired to Paris. But, of course, it is wrong to laugh at the opposition to steam. Nowadays, nothing could have quite the daunting novelty of steam with its half-religious implications – the first and only source of power that did not derive from muscles, the wind or falling water.

Brunel, and probably other people, produced the immediate answer to the reverend doctor: the power needed to drive a ship was roughly proportional to the square of its main dimensions but the amount of coal it could carry was proportional to the cube. Therefore, the larger the

THE EDITOR OF 'THE CABINET CYCLOPEDIA'.

Rev. Dr. Dionysius Lardner, a professor at University College, London, was a vocal, influential and singularly ill-informed early critic of steamships.

ship, the greater its range, and there was no limit to the range if you built the ship large enough. The long-term answer, of course, was to make the engines more efficient but that took time. Especially, it had to wait for the invention of steel. The first iron boilers could only be built to stand a pressure of about 5 lb per square inch, and with steam at that pressure no engine could be efficient.

Thus it was the Merchant Navy, not the Royal Navy, which did all the pioneering of steam – the designing, improving, experimenting, the occasional expensive mistakes, and above all the organizing and administration of steam fleets. They did not consciously do it to rescue the Empire from its crisis. Their motives were purely commercial – to make a profit. But in doing it, they tided the Empire over its time of crisis, so that when the Royal Navy in the end had to change its mind, 20 to 30 years of work were already accomplished and available for it to use.

The reason why the Merchant Navy was so keen on steam was revealed by those Willcox and Anderson advertisements. Their company's steamers, they announced, would start from London every Friday and from Falmouth every Monday. The average times for the passages would be from Falmouth to Vigo 54 hours, to Lisbon 84 hours, and to Gibraltar, including a 24-hour stop at Lisbon and six hours at Cadiz, seven days. This regular timetable was something entirely new in sea travel. No passenger under sail had ever known when his ship would leave, let alone when it might arrive, and if he asked, the answer was always 'wind and tide permitting'. The most remarkable thing, to a traveller in that era, was the confident prediction of a mere weekend from London to Falmouth. That had always been an awkward journey, needing a westerly wind to get out of the Thames, then an easterly one all the way down the English Channel. It had been a common practice, through all the centuries of sail, to drift down the Channel with the ebbing tide and anchor when it turned, and that part of the voyage might have taken anything up to ten days.

By 1837 Willcox and Anderson were nearer their dream of a regular service. Outwardly, they were full of confidence, however much they were inwardly haunted by the thought that they were losing money and that most of the richer and grander people trying to do the same thing were facing bankruptcy. They were sure a regular service would be welcomed by passengers and by merchants who had cargoes to ship. Anderson knew the Portuguese and Spanish coasts very well and he had learned to speak Spanish. The only remaining problem was to make it pay.

Probably the answer to that came from a very useful ally who had joined them in 1835, called Richard Bourne. He was an ex-naval captain and his family held the Government contract to distribute the overland mails by coach in Ireland. They also ran a steamship line, the Dublin and London Steam Packet Company. It was Bourne who provided most of the ships that Willcox and Anderson used – *William Fawcett* was one – and he certainly knew that the way to turn a loss to a profit was to win a mail contract. So they began to press the authorities for a contract to carry the mails to Portugal and Spain.

It was not so difficult as it might have been because the packets (as the

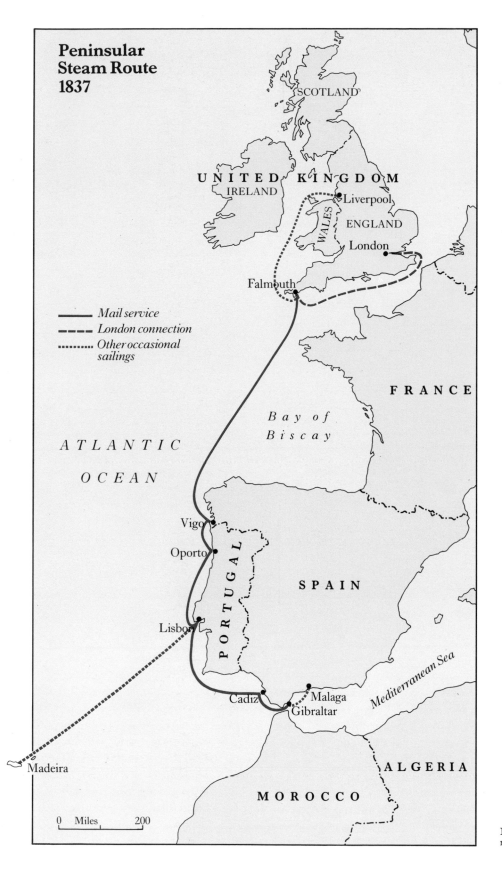

Peninsular Steam Route 1837

SCOTLAND

UNITED KINGDOM
IRELAND

Liverpool

WALES ENGLAND

London

Falmouth

FRANCE

Bay of Biscay

ATLANTIC

OCEAN

——— Mail service
– – – London connection
········· Other occasional sailings

Vigo

Oporto

P O R T U G A L

S P A I N

Lisbon

Cadiz
Malaga
Gibraltar

Mediterranean Sea

Madeira

ALGERIA

MOROCCO

0   Miles   200

Map of the Peninsular Steam mail service in 1837.

Captain Richard Bourne,
R.N. (*c.*1787–1850), Dublin
shipowner and owner of the
William Fawcett who joined
forces with Willcox &
Anderson in establishing
Peninsular Steam Navigation
Company.

mail ships were called), which had been run by the Post Office but were being taken over by the Admiralty, had a very bad reputation. Those to Spain and Portugal were sailing ships and often took three weeks to get to Lisbon. They were inefficient and corrupt. Their captains did not always bother to go to sea but sat at home and drew their pay while the ships were commanded by seamen whose navigation was erratic, and the crews of the transatlantic packets were allowed to trade on their own account. Their ambition was, therefore, to be captured by privateers, when they happily threw the mails overboard and made a good living by bogus insurance claims for imaginary trade goods. It was noticed that packets were captured much more often than any other ships; thus merchants whose business depended on regular mails were all in favour of handing them over to good commercial carriers.

Nevertheless, when Willcox and Anderson made a proposal for improving things it was 'coldly received and disregarded' by the Admiralty. The merchants complained ever more loudly and the Lords Commissioners at last relented and said it was willing to listen. The partners submitted a more detailed proposal, with an estimate of £30,000 a year, which was a lot less than the old arrangement was costing. The Admiralty accepted the proposal but said they were going to call for tenders for carrying it out.

Only one competing tender was made, by a rival company called Commercial Steam Navigation, but it could not satisfy the Government that it had the ships or organization required. So Willcox and Anderson, in the name of their new company, won the contract to carry the mails, with a regular income they knew would make all the difference between loss and profit, failure and success. The contract was signed by Richard Bourne on 22 August 1837, which is the date accepted for the founding of P&O. The first ship sailed under it on 1 September. She was the *Don Juan*, the largest of the fleet, and Arthur Anderson sailed with her, this time taking his wife, Mary Ann: a proud and happy moment, one imagines, for them both. A fortnight later, they met disaster.

Anderson himself told the story in a long letter to Lloyds' agent at Gibraltar. They left Gibraltar for their voyage home, with the homegoing mail on board and $21,000 in cash, and soon after they ran into thick fog. Anderson had been on deck talking to the captain, whose name was John Engledue. When dusk was falling he went down to his cabin, 'where I had only been a few minutes when I heard Captain

Richard Bourne initialled the first Mail Contract on 22 August 1837. This gave Peninsular Steam a regular income to bolster its faltering fortunes, and has by tradition been considered the founding of the company renamed P&O three years later.

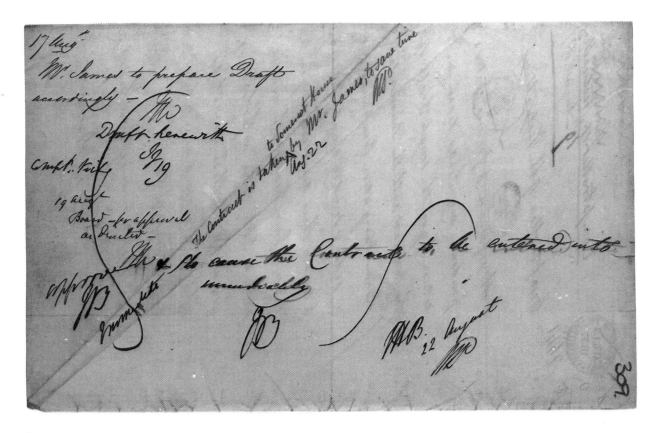

Engledue calling out loudly, "Hard a starboard. Stop her. Back her." I immediately rushed on deck, and saw a ledge of rocks about 40 yards or so from the starboard bow, with Tarifa lighthouse at a short distance. She touched very gently forwards, carrying away as she grazed the rocks, the starboard paddleboards. The boats were immediately lowered away; a large kedge was carried out on the starboard quarter, a strong hawser passed from it abaft, a tackle put on, and everyone on board set on to endeavour to heave her off. These efforts were, however, in vain . . .'

Anderson hired a Spanish fishing boat which had turned up to see what was happening, and set off to go back to Gibraltar with his wife, two passengers and Lieutenant Roupel the Admiralty Messenger. 'We did not get to Gibraltar until one o'clock of the morning, completely drenched through.' There they saw Captain Austin of the packet HMS *Medea*, who got up steam ready to go to the assistance of *Don Juan*, and visited his commanding officer, Captain Fisher of HMS *Asia*, who lent them a carpenter and his crew for stopping leaks and a party of marines to protect the ship from plunder. With the chartered schooner *Lady Newman* in tow, they set off for the wreck.

'We arrived at Tarifa, thus provided, about six o'clock in the morning. I found my apprehensions, from the rapid manner in which the vessel was making water when I left her, (in consequence of a sharp rock which lay under her starboard bow) but too well grounded. She

Tarifa, the southern Spanish town that saw the wreck of *Don Juan* on the first northward mail sailing on 15 September 1837, an event which could easily have spelled disaster for the Peninsular company. (Watercolour from *Route of the Overland Mail to India*, 1850)

had settled so far that her cabin port sills were scarcely clear of the water; the masts, funnel, and part of the starboard paddlebox being the only parts of the vessel visible.'

They spent the rest of the night in a furious discussion with the governor of Tarifa: in the course of it, Captain Austin threatened to avenge the 'insult to the British flag by battering down their walls about their ears'. But it ended in a friendly fashion, and next day HMS *Medea* left for England, taking the mails and Captain Engledue. Anderson stayed behind to report on the state of the wreck. 'On the outside,' he wrote, 'there is 18 fathoms depth of water, and but for the strong way in which Captain Engledue secured it by passing the chain cables round a rock, I think the vessel would have fallen over and sunk in this deep water.' In short, there was no hope of saving anything from the *Don Juan* except the mails and the cash, and most luckily everybody's life.

2

ONWARDS TO INDIA

Everything happened so quickly in those early days of P&O, that one cannot always discern what Willcox and Anderson were thinking and how far their secret ambitions were running ahead of events. In the first few months, it seems unlikely they had thought of going any farther than Spain and Portugal, with Gibraltar as their final port. Possibly, an extension through the Mediterranean to Malta, Alexandria in Egypt, Corfu and even Constantinople in Turkey, was in their minds, but they cannot yet have dreamed they might go to India and beyond, or that their humble company might become an essential part of the British Empire's power.

On his way home from the loss of the *Don Juan*, Anderson must have believed that it was all over, that whatever dreams they had were ended. Their biggest ship was a total loss and it was only partly insured (a mistake they never made again). That was bad enough; it was worse that the reputation they had hoped to win now seemed to be hopelessly lost. What would Willcox, or Richard Bourne, say when he brought them the news? Would they decide they had to stop and put the new company into liquidation? And the Post Office: would it withdraw the contract? One hopes his wife was able to cheer him up on the long voyage back to Falmouth.

It seemed obvious then, and still seems obvious now, that the loss of the ship was the fault of Captain Engledue. Tarifa is the southernmost point of Spain, where a ship from Gibraltar or the Mediterranean, bound for northern Europe, begins its turn to starboard. The Captain had started his turn too soon or else had been steering too northerly a course from Gibraltar. Fog or not, he had broken the most elementary rule of pilotage:

> *Outward bound,*
> *Don't run aground.*

But Anderson was not a censorious man and his letter ended: 'An error of this nature, even if there was one, surely ought to be judged with leniency, and whoever is aware of Captain Engledue's feelings under his misfortune will, if he have a spark of generosity in his bosom, be more disposed to administer the balm of sympathy and consolation than to aggravate his distress by thoughtless or illiberal censure.'

Richard Bourne confirmed what Anderson said and consequently Captain Engledue did not lose his ticket or his job. On the contrary, the company promoted him. He lived another 51 years and when he died in 1888 he was a director and the last survivor of the pioneers.

In general, the result of this disaster was the opposite of Anderson's fears. People did not blame the young company but treated it with

(*Opposite above*)
Don Juan was wrecked in fog. Heavy weather was also a hazard for steamers, but more so for sailing ships. P&O's 450-ton *Liverpool* (built in 1832) came to the rescue of the Dutch vessel *Banka* off the Portuguese coast in 1845.
(Oil by W.J. Huggins)

(*Opposite below*)
Before 1840, Peninsular Steam's mail sailings went only as far as Gibraltar. Admiralty steam packets operated along the length of the Mediterranean, and East India Company ships beyond the Isthmus of Suez.
(Watercolour by A. Nicholl, 1841)

P&O's sailings from Southampton to Alexandria stopped only at Gibraltar and at Valetta, the harbour of Malta. In later years fast connections from Malta to Marseilles enabled passengers in a hurry to save time by crossing through France.
(Watercolour from *Route of the Overland Mail to India*, 1850)

'sympathy and consolation'. Passengers still came for tickets. Even the Admiralty seemed impressed to learn that the very first thing Anderson had done while the ship was sinking was to rescue the mail and send it through with hardly a day's delay. Far from cancelling the contract, within less than a year it invited the two men to make plans for taking the mail further, from Gibraltar right through the Mediterranean to Alexandria in Egypt.

At that stage, the two men's ambition must have begun to widen, not only to the Mediterranean but far beyond. The importance of Alexandria was not the mail or trade to Egypt itself; it was the next staging post for the mail to India, which went across the isthmus of Suez, a slow and sometimes dangerous desert journey on donkey and camel back, to be picked up by other ships in the Red Sea. Suddenly, there was a glimpse of the vast horizons of the far eastern Empire.

First, though, the Mediterranean. The plan that Willcox and Anderson proposed was a line of large steamers to run direct from England to Alexandria, calling only at Gibraltar and Malta. Several companies put in tenders but the two men won the contract with a bid of £34,200 a year for five years.

There was a particular reason for using the fastest possible ships and the fewest possible stops: they had to compete with an overland route which was bound to be faster. Part of the mail to Alexandria already went by sea: Willcox and Anderson took it to Gibraltar, and Government packets took it on from there. But part of it went by coach through France to Marseilles, and only from there by sea.

However the British Government did not like to trust the French with its diplomatic mail. It was 25 years since the Napoleonic wars had ended at Waterloo, but before that France had been the national enemy for longer than most people could remember. The French, in fact, never interfered with the mail, but it was uncomfortable to think that all through France it was at the mercy of any highwayman. Therefore speed was not the only thing that mattered. To the Government, it was also important that Willcox and Anderson offered to take the mail in British ships, stopping only at British ports.

To take on this extension, the company had to grow, very quickly. Before it could grow, it needed to be incorporated by Royal Charter, which brought the advantage of limited liability. It received its charter in December 1840, with a large new Court of Directors, including Willcox and Anderson as Managing Directors, and an authorized capital of £1 million. The new service demanded two large ships and to satisfy the mail contract they had to be 'fit and able to carry and fire at least four guns of the largest calibre now used on any of Her Majesty's steam vessels of war'. In exchange for shares, the company acquired one ship from a transatlantic company which had run into difficulties (like many others) when Samuel Cunard won the transatlantic mail contract.

Under the 1840 contract P&O's 'Oriental' extension stopped at Alexandria, but within two years it had become just a staging post on a P&O service all the way to India.
(Watercolour by A. Nicholl, 1840)

25

To open its Mediterranean service, P&O needed larger ships than before. One was the Atlantic steamer *Liverpool* which was purchased, refitted, enlarged (to 1,600 tons) and renamed *Great Liverpool* to avoid confusion with the smaller *Liverpool* already in the P&O fleet (see page 22). (Lithograph by J.I. Herdman after N.J. Kemp, 1840)

Built for the Atlantic, P&O renamed her the *Great Liverpool*; and they bought another, still on the stocks, and named her the *Oriental*.

The *Oriental* was the first of these two to steam to Alexandria. She was probably the biggest ship that had ever called at that port; certainly, she was the most comfortable, because she was completed to the design of P&O, and its standard of passenger comfort was already high.

History does not tell whether Anderson sailed on the *Oriental*'s maiden voyage. He probably did; he seldom missed such a chance. He was certainly in Egypt in the following year, 1841, and he must have pondered then on the narrow strip of sand, hardly 150 miles across, which separated him and his ship from the Red Sea and the thousands of miles of open ocean beyond: to Bombay, Ceylon, Calcutta, China, Australia. It is only surmise that this appealed to his ambition, but it is a fact that the company had given an undertaking, in its charter, that within two years it would run a steam service from Egypt to India, that no mail contract had yet been agreed, and that even Anderson, the practical man of the company, had no very clear idea how to do it.

Of course, there were two routes to India and everything beyond: the route across those 150 miles of desert, down the Red Sea and across the Indian Ocean, and the much longer but uninterrupted route round the Cape of Good Hope. Discovery of the Cape route is attributed to Vasco da Gama in 1498, though there are stories of early Greek navigators who disappeared through the Strait of Gibraltar and turned up again, years later, at the mouth of the Red Sea, having followed the shore all the way.

The Suez route was much more ancient; parts of it were the oldest trade route in the world. King Solomon used it, 1,000 years before Christ, to search for the riches of Ophir: his ships were built in the Gulf of Aqaba, south of Suez, and his sailors were Phoenicians who trekked across from the Mediterranean shore.

But even King Solomon was following a route which was already ancient. For 1,500 years before him, the Sumerians had been sailing the parallel route, from Babylon and Ur down the Persian Gulf, and bringing back the goods he coveted, gold, copper, ivory, rare woods and precious stones, even apes and peacocks. The two routes joined at the southern end of the Red Sea and the Gulf, and continued together down the coasts of Africa and India. This part of the route had, therefore, been in use for 4,500 years.

The leading navigators on it were the Arabs, who sailed the kind of dhow called a boom, which is still built in the Gulf, though not in the Red Sea. The secret of their navigation, which they had always tried to hide from their rivals, was the seasonal variation of the monsoon wind – a steady southwest wind from May to September and a steady northeaster from October to April. With that wind they were certain of making one round voyage a year, outward and back; but more than one voyage a year was impossible.

One Empire after another, as they rose and fell, had used the route: among them the Sumerians, Romans, Greeks, Chinese, Egyptians, the Arabian Empire itself at the time of the Prophet, the Portuguese and

First P&O ship to sail to Alexandria was the 1,787-ton *Oriental*, bought on the stocks in 1840 and originally intended for North Atlantic service. Her career ended when she was broken up at Hong Kong in 1861. (Deck plan from Captain James Barber's *Overland Guide Book*, 1845)

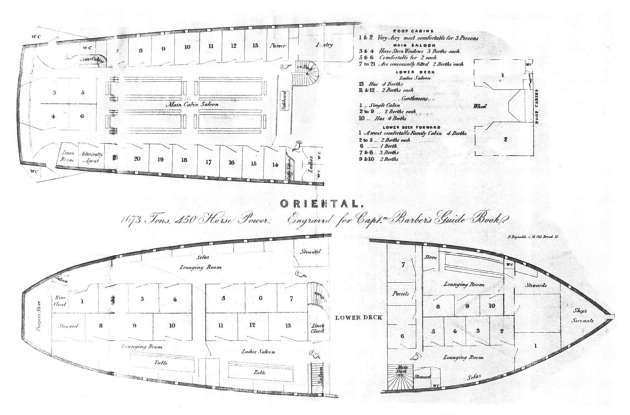

27

Dutch, and then the British. Of course, the secret had been learned by European navigators of the sixteenth century, but through all the millennia of sail the monsoon had been both its motive power and its limitation – one round voyage a year. It was still the same. This seemed to the advocates of steam a golden opportunity: at last, to beat the monsoon.

In 1840, when P&O reached Alexandria, people had been talking of using steam in the east, and even trying it for 20 years, but nobody had really succeeded. Anderson, looking out across the sands of Suez, was probably perfectly confident he could beat a monsoon: it was only the technical problem of building ships that were big enough and powerful enough to make a reasonable speed against a head wind. But he must also have known that if his ships ever reached the other side of that barrier of sand, he would be up against an immensely rich and well-established human rival: the East India Company.

P&O's charter was a few weeks old: the East India Company's dated back to 1600, when Queen Elizabeth I granted it a monopoly of trade beyond the Cape of Good Hope and Cape Horn. In the time of Charles II, it had risen in power until it had the right to 'acquire territory, coin money, command fortresses and troops, form alliances, make war and peace, and exercise civil and criminal jurisdiction'. In short, the commercial company was the *de facto* government of India. But in the early part of the nineteenth century, its power had waned and it had been deprived of its monopolies one by one. In 1840 – though nobody

In the mid-nineteenth century trade south from Suez was dominated by Arab navigators in their traditional dhows. Steamers took away the cream of the trade, but today there are still dhows throughout the Middle East.

East Indiamen were built for comfort, not speed. In the 1830s they were succeeded by the faster 'Blackwall frigates' such as R&H Green's *Madagascar*, but even they were unable to get their passengers to and from India faster round the Cape than P&O's steamers linked by the Overland Route.

foresaw this – it had only 18 more years to live until the Indian Mutiny so exposed its malpractices that all its powers were surrendered to the Crown.

During its centuries of existence, it had built a fleet of ships, the East Indiamen, which connoisseurs of shipbuilding considered the aristocrats of the shipping world. Most of them were built in the Blackwall yard adjoining the East India Dock on the Thames; but some were built in the East, entirely of Burma teak, which is the best shipbuilding timber in the world – for only the best was good enough. The East Indiamen were stately, ornate and magnificent, but they were built for comfort, even luxury, not for speed – and they were not steam ships. They were still limited by the monsoon and the round voyage to England by way of the Cape commonly took most of a year. That was a great hardship for the thousands of Englishmen the East India Company employed as civil servants or soldiers. They were exiles; if they wrote a letter home, they had to wait a year for an answer. Yet the Company was half-hearted in experiments in steam. Its enemies said it did not want to be in close touch with England, for fear of losing its independence. Most of the talk about steam was not due to the Company but to separate groups or committees of British or Indian businessmen. It had rarely gone beyond talk, but the voyage of the steamer *Enterprize* from London to Calcutta in 1821 was part of it. It was hoped the *Enterprize* would make the voyage in 70 days but, in fact, she took 103, which was not much quicker than the East Indiamen under sail, and the experiment was written off as a failure.

Other attempts were made on the Red Sea route but with no more success. In 1829, the East India Company itself built a steamer in Bombay called the *Hugh Lindsay*, which was intended to run between Bombay and Suez, but she was so inadequate that she only strengthened the argument that the Company was not really trying and did not want a quicker route to Britain. The longest leg of that voyage was from

Bombay to Aden, 1,710 miles. At her best speed it was calculated she might do it in 10 or 11 days, but she was built with only a coal capacity for 5½ days. She left Bombay with even her passenger saloon and cabins so full of coal that her decks were almost awash. She did make it to Aden, using sail whenever she could; spent six days there extracting more coal from the Sultan; staggered on to Mocha and Jedda and finally reached Suez after just over a month, with her speed down to 3 knots when the monsoon was against her. With one or two other experimental ships, she carried on running from Bombay to Suez for many more years, but never made more than one round voyage a year – no more than sailing ships had been doing for centuries.

For reasons that were obscure and political, the East India Company refused to give up its monopoly of that route, the shortest to England. But it did agree to let P&O try another longer route: from Suez and Aden down to Ceylon and then up the other side of India to Madras and Calcutta.

The undertaking P&O had given, under the terms of its charter, was sufficiently vague. It had only promised, within two years, to run a service from Suez to India – and it had not said what part of India. This was the problem which confronted Anderson and the other members of the Board: to provide two ships, very quickly, big enough and powerful enough to defy the monsoon, and comfortable enough to satisfy passengers who were used to the luxury of the old East Indiamen.

Financially, it remained a leap in the dark. The large new ships would cost at least £60,000 each, with perhaps another £10,000 each to take them to their station in Calcutta. Nobody had offered to pay for them, and as ever they would not pay for themselves unless they could win a mail contract – which seemed unlikely, for most of the mail would probably go to Bombay, rather than Calcutta. There was an uneasy feeling that the East India Company was waiting expectantly to see the newcomers fail. It was true it had offered to pay P&O £20,000 a year if it made four round voyages in the first year, six in the second and one a month in the next three. But as the East India Company itself had tried and failed to make one journey a year on the shorter route to Bombay, that offer looked like a bet that it was sure it would win.

Undaunted, P&O ordered the two biggest ships it had ever considered, wooden paddlers 240 feet long, one just under and the other just over 2,000 tons. They had iron watertight bulkheads for safety and 60 cabins and 150 berths, but both had engines of conservative design, because reliability in those distant seas was reckoned more important than fuel economy. The first they named *Hindostan*, and the second *Bentinck*, after Lord William Bentinck, a governor of India who had encouraged the Company in its early days.

They were elegant ships, three-masters with two tall white funnels each, clipper bows, long bowsprits and stern windows like early warships. Newspapers were full of praise for their luxury – genteel, superb, magnificent, commodious – and were especially impressed by their 'warm, cold and shower baths'; indeed it was something new to be offered such comforts at sea.

Hitherto, passenger steamers had been built with a saloon in the

(*Opposite above*) *Hindostan* (2,018 tons) leaving Southampton on her maiden voyage on 24 September 1842; she sailed round the Cape to Calcutta and there commenced sailings to and from Suez, via Point de Galle and Aden, to connect with passengers travelling by P&O to Alexandria.

(*Opposite below*) *Hindostan* and her sister *Bentinck* were powerful enough to beat the monsoon and comfortable enough to compete with the East India Company's steamers south from Suez or sailing ships round the Cape. (Deck plans from Captain James Barber's *Overland Guide Book*, 1845)

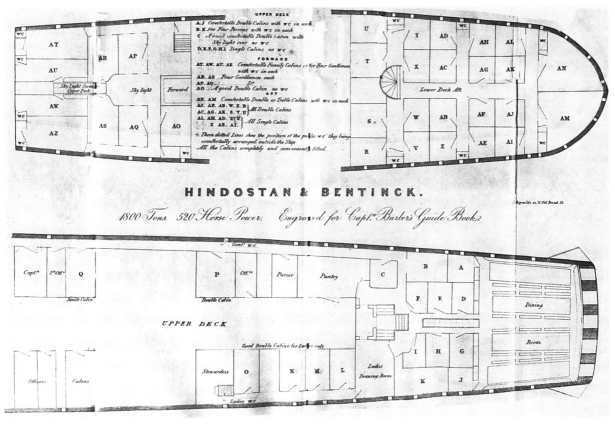

HINDOSTAN & BENTINCK.

1800 Tons. 520 Horse Power. Engraved for Captᵗⁿ Barber's Guide Book

middle, and cabins opening off it either side – an arrangement which can still be seen in the rebuilt *Great Britain* now on view in the Great Western Dock at Bristol. P&O reversed that plan, building their saloons the full width of the ship in the stern, and forward of it two passages, one either side of the ship, with a double row of cabins between them. The theory was that passengers in these cabins would not be so much affected by the rolling of the ship and would not hear the water rushing

Published under the Her Majesty's

Authority of Postmaster General.

DAILY PACKET LIST.

GENERAL POST OFFICE.
[FHB]

No. 15,906   SATURDAY, NOVEMBER 3, 1849.

DAILY STATEMENT OF THE PACKET BOATS.

Stations.	Destinations.	Made up in London.	When due in London.	Mails Arr.	Date.	Mails due.
Dover	Calais	Twice daily, Sunday except	Twice daily, Sunday except	2 – 1 Yesterd.	—	—
	Ostend	Every day Sunday exceptd	Daily	1 Yesterday	—	—
The Thames	Holland	Wed. & Sat. Morning.	Monday & Thursday	—	—	—
	Hamburg	Tuesday and Friday	Tuesday & Saturday	—	—	—
Holyhead	Dublin	Twice daily	Sunday	2	1 2	—
Port Patrick	Waterford	Every day	excepted	1	1	—
Southampton	Jersey & Guernsey	Mon. Wed. & Friday Even.	Tues. Thurs. & Saturd.	1	2	—

SOUTHAMPTON STATION.

Destinations.	Mails dispatched from London.	Last Packets Sailed from Southampton.	Next Packet due at Southampton.	Arr. at Southampton and Date of Mails.
Lisbon, Spain, and Gibraltar	7th, 17th, & 27th of every Month. (By Day Mail.)	MONTROSE .... Oct. 27	Next Mail due .. Nov. 6	
Gibraltar, Malta, Greece, & Ionian Islds	20th of every Month.	RIPON........... Oct. 20	Next Mail due Nov. 28	
Egypt, Ceylon, India, and China				CLYDE. (Mails arrived Yesterday).
(1) British Colonies in West Indies, (EXCEPT HONDURAS, NASSAU & BERMUDA)				Santa Martha .... Sep. 19
Foreign Colonies in W. Indies (EXCEPT HAVANA,)	2d and 17th of every Month.	THAMES .... Nov. 2	Next Mail due Nov. 22	Chagres & Panama.—25&28 Demerara ....Oct. 5 Santiago de Cuba.. — 6
Venezuela, & Jacmel				La Guayra .... — 7
(2) Bermuda, Nassau New Orleans, Mexico Honduras, & Havana	2d of every Month only.	THAMES .... Nov. 2	Next Mail due Nov. 22	Jamaica .... — 8 Grenada .... — 9 Barbadoes .... — 10
(3) Madeira, GreyTown (S. JUAN DE NICARAGUA) & New Granada, Chili & Peru	17th of every Month only.	MEDWAY .... Oct. 17	Next Mail due .. Nov. 22	Antigua .... — 11 St. Thomas ...... — 14 Carthagena ..... no date Jacmel .... no date

FALMOUTH STATION.

Destinations.	Mails dispatched from London.	Last Packet Sailed from Falmouth.	Next Packet due at Falmouth.	Arr. at Falmouth and date of Mails
Madeira Brazil Buenos Ayres	Evening of 4th of every Month.	HMB LINNET ...... Oct. 6	H.M.B. EXPRESS Nov. 24	

LIVERPOOL STATION.

Destinations.	Mails dispatched from London.	Last Packet sailed from Liverpool.	Next Packet due at Liverpool.	Arr. at Liverpool and dat of Mails.
British North America, and United States.	Every alternate Friday in December, January, February, and March, and every Friday during the remainder of the year.	CAMBRIA .... Oct. 27	CALEDONIA .. Nov. 7	

NOTICE. — H.M. Sloop "SERPENT," with Mails for Rio de Janeiro, will not sail from Portsmouth before the 4th inst. Letters for Rio de Janeiro may be posted in London up to this Evening, and will be liable to a postage of 2s. 9d. the half ounce, and so on; no charge will be made upon Newspapers.

NOTICE —— H.M. Sloop WOLVERINE, with Mails for Madeira, Cape de Verde Islands. Sierra Leone, and Ascension, sailed from Devonport on the Morning of 2nd inst.

VIGO OPORTO LISBON CADIZ GIBRALTAR MEDITERRANEAN EGYPT INDIA AND CHINA.

JUPITER, for the Peninsula &c., Mails of the Morning of 7th inst.

The next Mails for GIBRALTAR, MALTA, GREECE, the IONIAN ISLANDS, EGYPT, INDIA, &c., via Southampton, will be despatched from hence on the Morning of 20th inst.

The next Mails for the Mediterranean, Egypt, India, &c., via Marseilles, will be despatched from hence on the Evening of 7th inst.

MADEIRA BRAZIL AND BUENOS AYRES.

H.M.B. PETEREL, for the Mails of the 5th inst.

[From *August* to *January* inclusive, the Packet touches at PERNAMBUCO and BAHIA on her *outward* passage to RIO JANEIRO, and the other Six Months on her *homeward*.]

WEST INDIES' &c

CLYDE, arrived, brought Passenger, Judge Scotland, Rev Mr. Roussilhe, Messrs. Lopez, Healley, Lataillade, Coman, Gardiner, Gomes, Hogg, Reid, Hyman (and child), Latimer, Roberts&Son, M'Nully, Eldridge, Evans and Conrad.

THAMES, sailed the 2nd inst., with all Letters for the West Indies, &c., that arrived, or were posted in London up to the Morning of that Day inclusive.

AMERICA.

AMERICA, with the Mails of the Evening of the 2nd inst., will sail on the arrival of that Night's Post at Liverpool.

CALEDONIA, for the Mails of the Evening of 9th inst, — to be conveyed to Boston.

HOLLAND AND HAMBURGH

RAINBOW, for the Holland Mails of this Morning.

JOHN BULL, with the Hamburgh Mails of the Evening of 2nd inst., sailed this Morning.

FRANCE & BELGIUM.

GARLAND, with French Mail of 1st inst., sailed 1st, at 11. 21. p.m. Pass. ALICE, with French Mail of 1st inst., sailed 1st, at 11. 20. p.m

TIME OF PUBLICATION 7 5

'Daily Packet List', for 3 November 1849, issued by the General Post Office and showing schedules of all the contract mail sailings. Government ships still carried some mail, but the commercial precedent set by Peninsular Steam's 1837 contract was spreading throughout the Empire.

past their ears. Furthermore, in tropical seas, the passages would insulate the cabins from the heat outside. It is hard to imagine that this was a great improvement but at least it showed that the company was thinking about its passengers' comfort.

The *Hindostan* sailed from Southampton in scenes of rejoicing on 24 September 1842. Sending a steamer on a long voyage still needed months of preparation. Somebody had to send coal ships under sail

SOUTHAMPTON STATION.

DESTINATION.	PACKETS.	CAPTAINS.	Malta, Mediterranean, Egypt, India, China, &c.	Spain, Portugal, & Gibraltar.	Date of Return.	Mails due.
Malta & Mediterranean Egypt, India, China, &c.	Ripon	Moresby	20 Oct.	—	—	—
	Indus	Soy	—	—	27 June	—
	Hindostan	Lewis	—	—	30 Oct.	—
Portugal, Spain, & Gibraltar. *Steamers.*	Pacha	W. Weeks	—	17 Oct.	—	8 Nov.
	Montrose	Bowen	—	27 Oct.	—	15 Nov.
	Iberia	—	—	—	4 Oct.	—
	Jupiter	Meshan	—	27 Oct.	—	—

			West Indies, &c. (1)	West Indies, &c. (2)	West Indies, &c. (3)	Date of Return.	Mails due.
West Indies, &c. Mexico, Chagres, New Granada, Venezuela. *Steamers.*	Great Western	Wolfe	2 June	2 June	—	—	—
	Conway	Onslow	17 July		17 July	—	—
	Tay	Chapman	17 Aug.		17 Aug.	—	—
	Teviot	Rivett	2 Sep.	2 Sep.	—	—	22 Nov.
	Avon	Hast	17 Sept.		17 Sept.	—	7 Dec.
	Dee	Allan	2 Oct.	2 Oct.	—	—	22 Dec.
	Medway	Symons	17 Oct.		17 Oct.	—	—
	Thames	Abbott	2 Nov.	2 Nov.	—	21 July	—
	Trent	Clarke	—	—	—	23 Sep.	—
	Severn	Vincent	—	—	—	20 Oct.	—
	Clyde	Moss	—	—	—	2 Nov.	—

FROM OTHER STATIONS.

STATIONS	PACKETS.	CAPTAINS.	Madeira, Brazil, & B. Ayres.	America	Calais & Ostend.	Holland	Hamburg	Date of Return.	Mails due.
	H.M B.								
Falmouth.	Express	Lowry	6 Aug.	—	—	—	—	—	24 Nov.
	Crane	Lewis	6 Sept.	—	—	—	—	—	24 Dec.
	Linnet	James	6 Oct.	—	—	—	—	—	24 Jan.
	Swift	Douglas	—	—	—	—	—	19 May	—
	Peterel	Creser	—	—	—	—	—	4 Sept.	—
	Seagull	Dicken	—	—	—	—	—	4 Oct.	—
	Penguin	Leslie	—	—	—	—	—	24 Oct.	—
Liverpool. *Steamers.*	Caledonia	Douglas	—	29 Sept.	—	—	—	—	7 Nov.
	Niagara	Stone	—	6 Oct.	—	—	—	—	15 Nov.
	Europa	Lott	—	13 Oct.	—	—	—	—	21 Nov.
	Hibernia	Lang	—	20 Oct.	—	—	—	—	29 Nov.
	Cambria	Leitch	—	27 Oct.	—	—	—	—	6 Dec.
	America	Shannon	—	—	—	—	—	22 Oct.	—
	Canada	Harrison	—	—	—	—	—	28 Oct.	—
	Asia	Judkins	—	—	—	—	—	—	—
	Africa	Ryrie	—	—	—	—	—	—	—
Dover. *Steamers.*	Vivid	Smithett	—	—	—	—	—	2 Oct.	—
	Garland	Aplin	—	—	1 Nov.	—	—	—	—
	Violet	Sherlock	—	—	—	—	—	1 Nov.	—
	Onyx	Raymond	—	—	—	—	—	2 Nov.	—
	Princess Alice	Scriven	—	—	1 Nov.	—	—	—	—
	Undine	Allen	—	—	—	—	—	30 Oct.	—
	Widgeon	Rutter	—	—	—	—	—	26 Oct.	—
Steamers from the Thames.	Princess Royal	Phillips	—	—	—	27 Oct.	—	—	—
	Ocean	Hast	—	—	31 Oct.	—	—	—	—
	John Bull	Corbin	—	—	—	3 Nov.	—	—	—
	Caledonia	Gibbs	—	—	31 Oct.	—	—	—	—
	Giraffe	Wade	—	—	15 Sept.	—	—	—	—
	Cntss. of Lonsdale	Stranack	—	—	—	24 Oct.	—	—	—
	Venezuela	Goodburn	—	—	—	—	—	—	—
	Columbine	Norwood	—	—	13 Oct.	—	—	—	—
	Sir Edward Banks	Balliston	—	—	—	—	—	—	—
	Rainbow	Stranack	—	—	—	—	—	1 Nov.	—
	Trident	Morris	—	—	—	—	—	4 Aug.	—
	Wilberforce	Finch	—	—	—	—	—	11 Aug.	—
	City of Hamburgh	Wade	—	—	—	—	—	—	—
	Menai	Stock	—	—	—	—	—	—	—

PRINTED AND PUBLISHED BY THE CONTRACTOR, FRANCIS SHANLY, 7, RED CROSS SQUARE, CRIPPLEGATE.
YEARLY SUBSCRIPTION, from the 16th of April, 1846, £1 2 6 TO BE PAID IN ADVANCE.

ahead of her to intermediate ports and agents had to arrange the drinking water and provisions. P&O had planned it well. The coal ships were ready and waiting in Gibraltar, St Vincent in the Cape Verde Islands, Ascension, Cape Town, Mauritius, Ceylon and Calcutta itself. The venture did not cost as much as they expected and the publicity filled her with passengers.

It must have been an enjoyable trip. Steam had given a freedom no ships had had before. Provided she called at the coaling ports, the *Hindostan* could pick her route. Sailing ships bound for the Cape had never gone the shortest way; they had kept well clear of the African coast to avoid the northgoing current there and had made their way southward close to the coast of South America, hoping to leave the Doldrums to port before they crossed due east to the Cape. The *Hindostan* could scorn such precautions: she set the most direct course from Cape Verde to Ascension, and from Ascension to Cape Town, and she thrashed her way at 10 knots through the Doldrums where ships in

P&O passengers could be very generous to officers whom they felt had given them good service. This vase was presented to Captain Samuel Lewis of *Hindostan* on her return to England for refit via the Cape in 1847.

all the history of the sea had lain becalmed. Beyond the Cape, she ran into heavy weather but made light of it, and she reached Calcutta after 63 days at sea and 28 in port, which was a satisfactory record.

As soon as the ship reached Calcutta, she was turned round to what was to be her regular route – Madras, Ceylon, Aden and Suez. She had had critics, who said she was bigger and more expensive than she need be, but she proved her power and size were needed to beat the monsoon. In August 1843, she logged 25 days and 3 hours from Calcutta to Suez, 4,787 miles, against the monsoon all the way, 'an ordinary monsoon voyage' said Robert Moresby, her captain, which he was confident of equalling, 'a few hours more or less', at any time of year.

As a regular route, the Cape could not compete with Suez because it was so much longer but P&O could now take the mails and passengers from England to India by the short route all the way, in the *Great Liverpool* or the *Oriental* from England to Egypt, and in the *Hindostan* or the *Bentinck* from Egypt to Calcutta. This speed and comfort transformed the lives of men who served in India, and their wives and families. But between the Mediterranean and the Red Sea, there was still that single gap: the 150 miles of sand from Alexandria to Suez.

Calcutta was the Indian destination for passengers and mails travelling with P&O. The East India Company retained a monopoly on the run to Bombay until 1854, although it did subsidize P&O's service until it obtained a mail contract between Suez and Calcutta in 1845. (Watercolour from *Route of the Overland Mail to India*, 1850)

(*Above*)
The two routes across Egypt
– to Suez or Cosseir – both
passed through desert.
Passengers on the latter route
saw the pyramids at Gizeh on
their journey up the Nile.
(Watercolour from *Old Cairo*
by David Roberts, 1845)

(*Right*)
On 3 May 1839 the Bishop of
Calcutta wrote to the Royal
Society for the Propagation
of the Gospel in London.
The letter went 'Care of Mr
Waghorn' and arrived on 8
July, a journey of 66 days.

3

OVERLAND VIA SUEZ

All through the 1830s and most of the 1840s, the history of that troublesome stretch of sand is full of the name of Thomas Waghorn. Waghorn was a young man, tough and resilient, who might have been called a self-employed courier. He was impatient as a traveller, a letter-writer and a lobbyist, and he was obsessed by the problems of getting mail to India as quickly as it could possibly be done – even if it was only a single bundle of letters that he could carry in his pocket. To knock off a day or two from any rival route he put himself to the hardship of exploring the quickest ways overland across Europe, and the route he advised was:

Ostende to Liège, by rail.
Liège to Aix la Chapelle, by coach.
Aix to Cologne, by rail.
Cologne to Mayence, by coach or Rhine boat.
Mayence to Basle, by steamer.
From Basle, by coach over the Alps to Venice.
Venice to Trieste, by steamer.

He had other suggestions: all the way down Italy by coach to Brindisi, or through France to Marseilles, mostly by coach, but including 150 miles by boat down the River Rhône. He judged these alternatives, not by how exhausting the journey might be, but by the reliability of the final crossing of the Mediterranean. His record from Bombay to England in 1834 or 1835 was 46 days, which he achieved by hiring a fast French brig in Alexandria, and sailing to Marseilles.

The crossing of Egypt gave him plenty of scope for his unusual passion. There were, and always had been since biblical times, two favourite routes. Both went from Alexandria to Cairo, partly by a very small canal. From Cairo, one went across the desert to Suez and the other went up the Nile to Luxor, and then across the desert to the small Red Sea port, 250 miles south of Suez, which was then called Cosseir and is now more pedantically spelt Quseir.

The route by Cosseir had the advantage of giving passengers a chance to see the ruins of Luxor, but the choice between them mainly depended on which way the monsoon was blowing in the Gulf of Suez, the narrow northern end of the Red Sea, and how strongly the current was flowing down the Nile. Both routes, if one may judge by travellers' stories, were extremely uncomfortable.

But one cannot be sure which stories to believe. Most of the passengers who went that way to India or back were British and one must admit they were either arrogant or boastful: did they hope to impress the readers of their letters and stories with their own fortitude, or surprise them with their patience? They ate and drank prodigiously, expected to be offered luxury, fiercely complained when they were not, and they treated all 'natives' with scorn and condescension. Perhaps the most evocative information comes from advice which was published in India by Waghorn, or by a rival of his called Hill. Northbound passengers were requested to write months in advance to say what ship they were coming on, and whether they would land in Suez or Cosseir. For parties by Cosseir, either Waghorn or Hill would engage donkeys, camels and Arab servants, and send a suitable number of boats up the river to Luxor. There were warnings. Every passenger must bring four or five dozen bottles of drinking water, and a supply of wine and spirits. As native bread was not edible, they should also bring biscuits or rusks. Some travellers added that all the food obtainable was impossible for Europeans to eat: 'the meat and chickens incredibly tough and tasteless and only the eggs eatably tender – if those boiled to leather or bullet consistency were resolutely rejected'. Other warnings may have come

Thomas Fletcher Waghorn (1800–49), indefatigable agitator for the fast carriage of mails to India, and pioneer of organized transit via the overland route across Egypt. (Oil by Sir George Hayter, 1844)

THE NILE-BOAT.

Before the advent of river steamers, passengers were transported up the Nile to Luxor in traditional Egyptian boats, frequently verminous in the extreme. (Engraving from Captain James Barber's *Overland Guide Book*, 1845)

from the rival couriers. Any boat provided at Luxor, for example, should be sunk for two or three days under the eyes of the traveller in the hope of killing its vermin; and even after that, the boat should be washed down once or twice a day with strong chloride of lime.

Both the couriers offered accommodation at Suez, which travellers said was a desert slum, and both ran 'omnibuses' on the desert crossings, horsedrawn six-seater covered wagons, and rest houses at places where travellers might be benighted. Perhaps the depth of discomfort was when the northbound passengers arrived outside Alexandria after the town gates had been shut for the night. 'In such case there was nothing for it but to resort to one of the low and villainous cafés and resorts outside the city walls, resolutely refuse to sit, much less lie down, and watch the locals lounge and scratch nonchalantly but non-stop.'

These stories give the impression that most mid-Victorians, even the few 'Livingstones' among them, were absurdly bad travellers who made things difficult for themselves by wearing unsuitable clothes, insisting on their own false dignity, refusing to eat anything that was not British, and treating the ladies among them with exaggerated care for their delicacy. One might have thought some would enjoy a glimpse of the desert but their only recorded pleasure was to look at ruins, and to leave the ladies in a hotel and find a vicarious thrill in watching the slave market of Cairo.

Waghorn always seems to have been surprised that travellers did not like his route. P&O was probably less surprised but it knew it would have to do something drastic to improve it. Most travellers assumed that P&O was in charge of it and their complaints poured in to the shipping company. There was a danger that if the reputation of Suez grew too bad, a substantial number of passengers – all those who were not in a hurry – would choose to go back to the slow but comfortable East Indiamen round the Cape. It was no use for P&O to say they were not in charge but Thomas Waghorn was. Waghorn said he was not: the Pasha of Egypt was in charge and if there were any shortcomings they were the

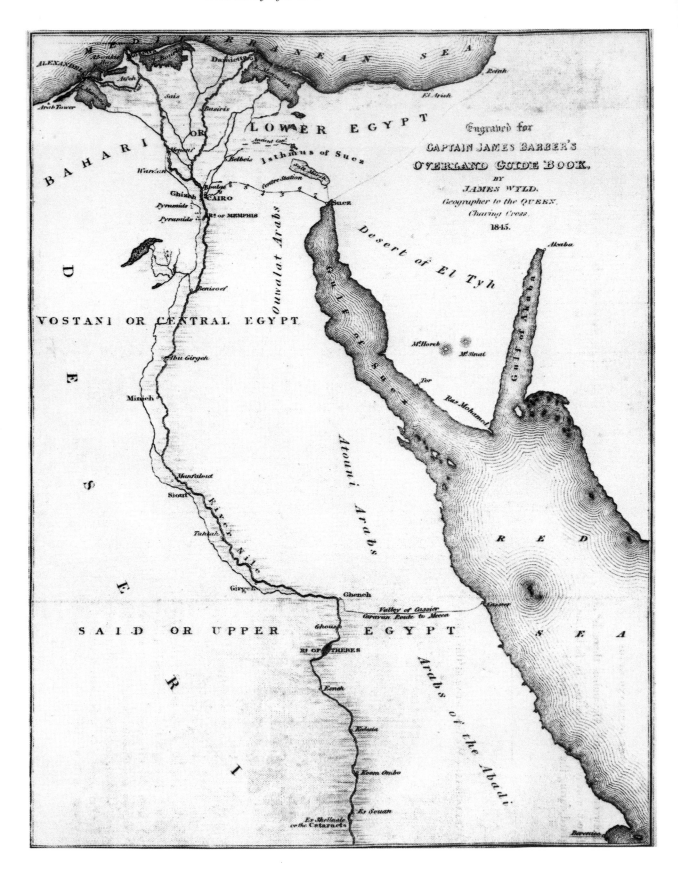

Pasha's fault. There was some truth in this, in so far as the Pasha had been an Albanian mercenary and was now a Muslim autocrat whose slightest whim was law in Egypt.

It took an external threat to unite all three of these parties. The threat to abandon the Suez route and return to the ancient Sumerian route down the Persian Gulf had happened once and could happen again. It had been feasible in biblical and pre-biblical times, and the British Government thought it could be done again. A Select Committee voted £30,000 to explore and survey a road in the neighbourhood of Aleppo to join the Mediterranean to the upper waters of the Euphrates, which seemed to be only 100 miles away. It might almost have worked but the border lands of Syria and Turkey were dangerous country, and the scheme was abandoned when one of the surveyors out on the job was murdered.

In the end, P&O had to intervene in Egypt, and once again, Anderson was sent to sort things out. He was helped by Captain Engledue, who had been promoted after he ran the *Don Juan* aground and was now Superintendent of the fleet of P&O.

(*Opposite*)
Map of the Overland Route across Egypt, 1845. (From Captain James Barber's *Overland Guide Book*)

(*Left*)
Mehemet Ali (*c.*1769–1849), the Albanian-born soldier who became Pasha of Egypt in 1806 and was much in favour of developing trading routes across the country because of the business it brought to Egypt. He was always on the friendliest terms with P&O, but the same could not be said of all his successors.
(Watercolour by John Frederick Lewis (1805–76))

Anderson was limited in what he could do because the company's charter only allowed it to act as a shipping company, not to run a route overland. First he persuaded Waghorn and Hill to pool their resources; and then he had many meetings with the Pasha, who was obliging and proposed to charge P&O ½ per cent of the value of goods that passed through his country, and also promised to improve the tracks that ran through the desert. The first part of both routes, starting from the north, from Alexandria to Cairo, used a canal 48 miles long which the Pasha himself had built a few years before by using 200,000 slaves. It was said to have been 9 feet wide and, in some parts, 18 feet deep – dimensions one would think impossible in sandy soil. It was used by native boats which were sailed or towed by horses and it was very slow. The boats which took passengers carried a trumpeter to warn others to clear the way, but they seldom did so and everything came to a halt while the tow ropes were lifted over the masts of boats that were coming the opposite way. Anderson improved the situation by getting some barges built, two for baggage and another two, with cabins and food and drink for his passengers, and finally a small steam tug to tow them.

Small though she was, that tug was revolutionary. She was named *Atfeh*, after the village where the canal joined the Nile, and she was the first iron ship P&O had ever built. She was also the first with twin screw propellers. There was a particular reason for building her of iron. She had to be built in England because there was nobody in Egypt who could build a tug. But she was not a seagoing ship and could not go to Egypt under her own steam. Therefore, she had to be assembled for her trials and then shipped to Egypt in pieces. That would not have been possible using wood but in iron it was achieved by assembling her with rivets made of lead and then melting the rivets out again.

Where that little canal joined the river at Atfeh of course there was a difference of level. All the baggage had to be lifted on to camels, carried 200 yards by them and lifted off into river steamers. The double handling caused complaints of damage, so Anderson built a lock which raised the canal boats and cut out the camels.

On the river itself, Waghorn had a steamer called the *Jack-o'-Lantern*, said to be the smallest passenger steamer in the world, and to be full of vermin. Anderson improved on her by adding two river steamers, the *Lotus* and the *Cairo*. The *Cairo* was larger, 100 feet in length and 14 feet in beam: the lightest possible iron shell, containing nothing but cabin space and an engine. Fifty men had berths below decks, and so did 16 ladies. The rest slept on deck under an enclosed awning. One would have thought the British were used to being under canvas but they had to be persuaded that in the Egyptian climate it was 'very agreeable for repose during the one night on the Nile'.

Finally, there were the desert crossings from Cairo to Suez or from Luxor to Cosseir. Nothing much could be done to improve them, but the Pasha did what he could with the tracks and Anderson did what he could with the horse-drawn omnibuses and the resthouses on the way. Between them, they cut down the time for that part of the journey to 36 hours, including 12 hours for rest and refreshment. It was not a very great hardship.

Indeed, the overall impression is that the dangers and discomforts of the crossing were exaggerated. The passengers were terrified of plague although there was no record of a passenger catching it. From their stories, one would have supposed they were exploring or pioneering but, in fact, the route was well-known and well-trodden. Apart from passengers, an enormous number of people and tons upon tons of cargo were always moving from one sea to the other. By 1846, 2,500 camels, 450 horses and uncounted donkeys were in regular use. If nothing else was in sight on the desert tracks, there was coal. A dump of 6,000 tons of coal had to be taken to Suez, because it was impossible to bring it in sailing ships up the Red Sea; it has been reckoned that that dump alone needed 18,000 camel journeys, a total of five million miles.

The most perceptive account of the omnibus journey was made by a young man in about 1856. He was only 20 and had recently joined the company, which was sending him to Hong Kong. His name was Thomas Sutherland – years later he became Chairman of P&O. He wrote:

> The road was merely a cutting in the sand, which in the night-time was not distinguishable from the desert itself. Indeed it was a very frequent occurrence for the horses to stray into the desert when the driver supposed he was in the middle of the road.
>
> A journey of some 18 hours under these circumstances could hardly be called enjoyable, even when the tedium was relieved by drinking innumerable cups of coffee, at the various stations where horses were changed. Still

The Mahmoudieh Canal, which Mehemet Ali had built by forced labour to link Alexandria to the Nile. Passengers and cargo travelled in barges towed by horses until P&O sent out a steam tug – their first iron and their first screw-driven vessel – in 1842. (Watercolour from *Route of the Overland Mail to India*, 1850)

River steamer off Boulac, the
port of Cairo. The journey up
from Atfeh, where the
Mahmoudieh Canal met the
river, took some fifteen to
twenty hours.
(Engraving from Captain
James Barber's *Overland
Guide Book*, 1845)

BOULAC.

(*Opposite above*)
The 'Central Station', one of
the series of stops for
refreshments (the food, it
was reported, was disgusting
and the beer was warm) and a
change of horses on the
desert crossing between
Cairo and Suez.
(Watercolour from *Route of
the Overland Mail to India*,
1850)

(*Opposite below*)
Suez, eastern end of the
desert crossing. P&O built
up an extensive Egyptian
establishment including coal
stocks (replenished
overland), hotel interests,
workshops, and farms for
fresh produce.
(Watercolour from *Route of
the Overland Mail to India*,
1850)

the experience was one which impressed the imagination in no ordinary
degree. A moonlight journey was most striking. The seemingly boundless
expanse, the silence only broken by the voice of the driver and the muffled
sound of the horses' feet (which seemed somehow to accentuate the sense of
stillness) the caravans loaded with mails and baggage passing with silent and
stealthy tread; the whitened bones of countless troops of camels, which had
died in harness, glistening in the moonlight; then the sudden daybreak, the
solitary Bedouin family mounted aloft on their desert ship, the mirage so
wonderful when first seen – these and other impressions remain indelible in
the minds of people who knew the Overland Route as it once was. Nor is it,
perhaps, the least vivid recollection that hardly more than a teacupful of
water could be obtained at Suez for the purpose of ablution after this weary
journey; unfiltered Nile water, which not the most ardent teetotaller would
have cared to drink had he been ever so thirsty. Needless to say that in those
days ice was unknown, and the draught of bottled beer which was usually
what the thirsty man fell back upon, tasted as if it had been three-fourths
mulled, and was followed by unrefreshing sleep, too frequently disturbed by
the stab of the mosquito or the furious assaults of all-pervading and insatiate
fleas.

However, there was one more snag that even Anderson could not
entirely overcome. Wherever a mail contract had been made with a
commercial firm, the Admiralty insisted it was nominally still in charge
of the mails and it sent a retired naval officer to look after them. Across
the Atlantic, that merely annoyed the officers of the ship: while they did
the work, the Admiralty officer had nothing whatever to do except eat
and drink, and some did too much of that. On the Eastern runs it was
more troublesome: the Admiralty man had authority to overrule the
Captain and order the ship to sail the moment the mails were on board.

It was possible for mails to cross from ship to ship in 64 hours, using

relays of donkeys and camels, and the Admiralty officer could order the ships to sail, whether the passengers had arrived or not. Hence it was conceivable that passengers, who had paid for their passage, could be stranded at Alexandria, or worse at Suez, until the next ship came in, and in the early days that might mean a month.

It took P&O a while to overcome this absurd anomaly and to persuade their passengers that they had done so, and that there was no risk of their being left behind in Egypt. Quite apart from the veto in the charter, none of this was really a job for a shipping company – neither to arrange, and much less to run, a crossing over land. Waghorn was always complaining at P&O's interference, and P&O was always explaining that it did not want to interfere: it was forced into it by the possible competition of the East Indiamen sailing round the Cape. Looking ahead, Anderson advised the Pasha to build a railway across the country, and P&O offered to lend him most of the cost of it. But those were early days even for a railway; it was scarcely 30 years since the Stockton and Darlington Railway was opened, and the Egyptian railway took so long to build that it was only finished shortly before the Suez Canal. Looking still further ahead, Anderson also talked of a canal. That idea had been in abeyance for some 50 years, since the Emperor Napoleon's surveyors had reported there was a difference of 30 feet in the levels of the Red Sea and the Mediterranean. Anderson checked their measurements and reported to Palmerston, the Foreign Secretary, that they were wrong. There was no difference and a canal was perfectly feasible. But still, as events turned out, a canal was 25 years in the future.

Mails carried by P&O were supervised by Admiralty Messengers, Naval officers with powers to see that contract requirements were fulfilled. Some were a thoroughgoing nuisance, others (as here) were apparently rather figures of fun.
(Sketch by William Thackeray from *Diary of a Voyage from Cornhill to Grand Cairo*, 1846)

4

CRUISING

As long ago as 1844, P&O invented deep-sea cruising. It seems once again that Anderson was the first with this novel idea – an entirely new use for ocean-going passenger steamers. He thought of it in 1835 before the new company was founded. At that time, among all his other ideas, he had started a newspaper called the *Shetland Journal* to inform his fellow-islanders of what was going on in the world. He published it himself, and seems to have written it too. In the first number, to fill up an empty space, he put in some dummy advertisements. One was for a mythical steamship to show tourists the wild, west coast of Shetland, and make round voyages to the Faeroe Islands and Iceland, and back to Shetland after a fortnight.

Anderson was always an optimist but it was surely carrying optimism too far if he hoped to find tourists to brave that voyage in the north Atlantic, even in summer, just for the pleasure of it. But nine years later in 1844, P&O took up the idea: not to the far north but round the Mediterranean. By then, they had a number of branch lines which connected with their regular ships to Alexandria, and they started to offer round tickets to Malta, Athens, Smyrna, Constantinople, Rhodes, Jaffa and Egypt and back to England, with shore excursions at each of the ports of call. On one of the first they gave a free ticket to the novelist W.M. Thackeray, and he wrote a book about the trip, using the *nom de plume* of Michael Angelo Titmarsh.

It is a curious little book, full of rather heavy-handed nineteenth-century humour. Thackeray was indebted to P&O and did his best to give a good impression of the pleasures of life at sea, but he seems to have found it hard work. Crossing the Bay of Biscay, all the passengers were seasick, including himself; and it was unexpectedly worse from Gibraltar to Malta. However, the kindly stewards who had been serving dinner were equally kindly in handing out basins, and:

> ... at last the indescribable moans and noises which had been issuing from behind the fine painted doors on each side of the cabin happily ceased. Long before sunrise I had the good fortune to discover that it was no longer necessary to maintain the horizontal posture, and, the very instant this truth was apparent, came on deck, at two o'clock in the morning, to see a noble full moon sinking westward, and millions of the most brilliant stars shining overhead.... The ship went rolling over a heavy, sweltering, calm sea. The breeze was a warm and soft one; quite different to the rigid air we had left behind us, off the Isle of Wight.

Unluckily, he did not like all he saw on shore. He hated Athens because, as he admitted, he had hated his classical education. He was 'abominably overcharged', he said, at the inn, and bitten all over by

The novelist William Makepeace Thackeray was given a free ticket by P&O on one of their first 'cruises' to the Mediterranean; he travelled on several ships – one to Gibraltar, another on to Greece and Constantinople, a third south to the Holy Land and Egypt – all running on normal commercial voyages rather than a 'cruise' in the modern sense. (Sketch by Daniel Maclise, 1832)

bugs. In his eyes, the city was a 'rickety agglomeration of huts'. He saw 'but two or three handsome women', and they had the great drawback of a 'sallow, greasy, coarse complexion. Dirty little children were playing about everywhere, with great big eyes, yellow faces, and the queerest little gowns and skull-caps.'

Smyrna and Constantinople pleased him more: at his first glimpse, the East seemed to him romantic. The timetable of the cruise gave him eight days in Constantinople, but he came away with what he called 'a remarkable catalogue of the things I didn't see'. Perhaps it would have been better if P&O had not given him his free ticket in the month of Ramadan, or Ramazan as he called it. As it was:

> I didn't see the dancing dervishes, it was Ramazan; nor the howling dervishes at Scutari, it was Ramazan; nor the interior of Saint Sofia, nor the women's apartments of the seraglio, nor the fashionable promenade of the Sweet Waters, always because it was Ramazan. On account of the same holy season the royal palaces and mosques are shut, the people remaining asleep all day, and passing the night in feasting and carousing.

On the way south towards Egypt the ship was due to call at Jaffa, and it picked up a deck cargo of pilgrims hoping to reach the Holy Land – Jews, Muslims and Christians. It was Thackeray's misfortune to scorn almost everything and everyone he saw that was not British, and he poured his adjectives on the pilgrims.

> In the cabin we were Poles and Russians, Frenchmen, Germans, Spaniards, and Greeks; on the deck were squatted several little colonies of people of different race and persuasions.... The dirt of these children of captivity exceeds all possibility of description: the profusion of stinks which they raised, the grease of venerable garments and faces, the horrible messes cooked in the filthy pots, and devoured with the nasty fingers, the squalor of

P&O's network of Mediterranean and Black Sea routes built up in the 1840's visited many ports such as Constantinople that were to be abandoned by the company as it concentrated on the Eastern mail services, but revisited when cruising began in earnest after 1904.
(Sketch by William Thackeray, frontispiece to his *Diary of a Voyage from Cornhill to Grand Cairo*, 1846)

A Street view at Constantinople

London. Published by Chapman & Hall, 186, Strand.

mats, pots, old bedding, and foul carpets of our Hebrew friends, could hardly be painted by Swift, in his dirtiest mood, and cannot be, of course, attempted by my timid and genteel pen.... Our attention was a good deal occupied in watching the strange ways and customs of the various comrades of ours. Once a week, on the eve before the Sabbath, there was a general washing in Jewry, which sufficed until the ensuing Friday. Among the women your humble servant discovered one who was a perfect rosebud of beauty, when first emerging from her Friday's toilette, and for a day or two afterwards, until each succeeding day's smut darkened those fresh and delicate cheeks of hers.... We had some very rough weather in the course of a passage from Constantinople to Jaffa, and the sea washed over and over our Israelitish friends and their baggages and bundles; but though they were said to be rich, they would not afford to pay for cabin shelter. One father of a family, finding his progeny half drowned in a squall vowed he *would* pay for a cabin; but the weather was somewhat finer the next day, and he could not squeeze out his dollars, and the ship's authorities would not admit him except upon payment.

One wonders what these indigenous people thought at their first sight of a young gentleman from fashionable London, but he only once offered a glimpse of himself.

As for the strangers, there is no need to describe them; that figure of an Englishman, with his hands in his pockets, has been seen all the world over: staring down the crater of Vesuvius, or into a Hottentot kraal, or at a pyramid, or a Parisian coffee house, or an Esquimaux hut, with the same insolent calmness of demeanour.

The visit to Jaffa should have been the climax of the cruise: from there the passengers rode to Jersusalem and Nazareth, the ladies

'Jerusalem from the Mount of Olives.' From Constantinople Thackeray sailed via Rhodes to Jaffa and thence rode to Jerusalem, but he was not impressed.
(Oil by Edward Lear, 1859)

THE ASCENT OF THE PYRAMIDS.

travelling in a sort of sedan chair slung between mules. But Thackeray, or Titmarsh, would not allow himself to be impressed by the Holy Places.

> The Church of the Sepulchre seems to me like a shabby theatre; I could get no better impression out of this the most famous church in the world. The deceits are too open and flagrant; the inconsistencies and contrivances too monstrous. The legends with which the Greeks and Latins have garnished the spot, have no more sacredness for you than the hideous, unreal, barbaric pictures and ornaments which they have lavished on it. The different churches battle for the possession of the various relics. The Greeks show you a tomb of Melchisedec, while the Armenians possess the Chapel of the Penitent Thief.... The place of the Invention of the Sacred Cross, the Fissure in the Rock of Golgotha, the Tomb of Adam himself – are all here within a few yards' space. You mount a few steps, and are told it is Calvary upon which you stand. All this in the midst of flaring candles, reeking incense, savage pictures of Scripture story, or portraits of kings who have been benefactors to the various chapels; a din and clatter of strange people – these weeping, bowing, kissing, those utterly indifferent; and the priests clad in outlandish robes, snuffing and chanting incomprehensible litanies, robing, disrobing, lighting up candles or extinguishing them, advancing, retreating, bowing with all sorts of unfamiliar genuflexions. Had it pleased the inventors of the Sepulchre topography to have fixed on fifty more spots of ground, as the places of the events of the sacred story, the pilgrim would have believed just as now. The priest's authority has so mastered his faith, that it accommodates itself to any demand upon it, and the English stranger looks on the scene, for the first time, with a feeling of scorn, bewilderment, and shame, at that grovelling credulity.

It is a pity P&O did not give the free ticket to a humbler, more tolerant and learned and less supercilious traveller; it would have been more interesting to know what those places and people were really like before tourism overwhelmed them. One does not even know whether Thackeray helped the idea of cruising to 'catch on'. Yet it was a legitimate

(*Above*)
Ships of the North of Scotland & Orkney & Shetland Steam Navigation Company were the first to begin cruises between Scotland and Norway, in 1886, reviving Arthur Anderson's ideas of some fifty years before.

(*Left*)
P&O began cruising in the modern sense in 1904. Even paperwork became more attractive once the passengers came by choice rather than necessity.

(*Opposite above*)
P&O's 'cruising yacht' *Vectis*
was converted in 1904 from
the liner *Rome* (built in 1881)
when she was no longer
needed for mail service. Not
until 1972 did P&O acquire a
ship built especially for
cruising.
(Gouache by R.H. Neville-
Cumming, 1904)

expansion. For the first time – certainly the first time since the Crusades – it offered a cheap and simple route for pilgrims from Britain to the Holy Land. It introduced Englishmen and women to the shores of the Mediterranean, where now they swarm. It created tourism. It may even have encouraged P&O in a similar but purely religious service farther East, where in the course of time, it became a principal means of transport for Muslim pilgrims from Pakistan and East Africa to Jedda, the port for Mecca.

In Egypt, of course, Thackeray climbed a pyramid, but made it a scene of his usual half-humorous grumbling.

> ... the swarms of howling beggars, who jostle you about the actual place, and scream in your ears incessantly and hang on your skirts, and bawl for money.... It was nothing but joking and laughter, bullying of guides, shouting for interpreters, quarrelling about sixpences.... You look up the tremendous steps, with a score of savage ruffians bellowing round you; you hear faint cheers and cries high up, and catch sight of little reptiles crawling upwards; soon a little jumping thing, no bigger than an insect a moment ago, bounces down upon you expanded into a panting major of Bengal cavalry. He drives off the Arabs with an oath, wipes his red, shining face, with his yellow handkerchief, and the next minute you see his nose plunged in a foaming beaker of brandy and soda-water. He can say now and for ever, he has been up the Pyramid.

In the Preface of his book Thackeray did acknowledge the kindness of P&O – partly, he said, to convince some incredulous friends who insisted he had never been abroad at all but had written the book 'out of pure fancy' in retirement at Putney. Looking back, he admitted it had been a delightful excursion. 'So easy, so charming, and I think profitable – it leaves such a store of pleasant recollections – that I can't but recommend all persons who have time and means to make a similar journey.'

P&O had to give up its Mediterranean cruises at the time of the Crimean War, and not much more is heard about cruising until the 1880s, when the *British Medical Journal* recommended sea voyages as curative. Perhaps encouraged by that, other owners bought the P&O *SS Ceylon* in 1881 and converted her into a 'cruising yacht', which sailed right round the world. In 1886 the North of Scotland and Orkney and Shetland Company, reverting to something like Anderson's first proposal, began a series of voyages to the Norwegian fiords in their *SS St Rognvald* (inclusive cost £10), and in 1889 the Orient Line began cruising to Norway and the Mediterannean. Both of these companies, Orient and North of Scotland, were later acquired by P&O, and in 1904 P&O itself converted a liner for cruising and renamed her *Vectis*. But even then, 60 years after Anderson thought of it, nobody could have foreseen that after two World Wars cruising would become the most constant and lucrative use for the largest, most famous liners.

Now it is still possible to take a P&O ferry to Shetland and, booking with a company for whom they are agents, follow Anderson's route to the Faeroes, Iceland, Norway and back.

(*Opposite below*)
Dining saloon aboard *Vectis*.
As *Rome* she carried 187
first- and 46 second-class
passengers, but on cruises
was restricted to 160 first-
class only. P&O was very
proud of the quality of the
new service it was offering.

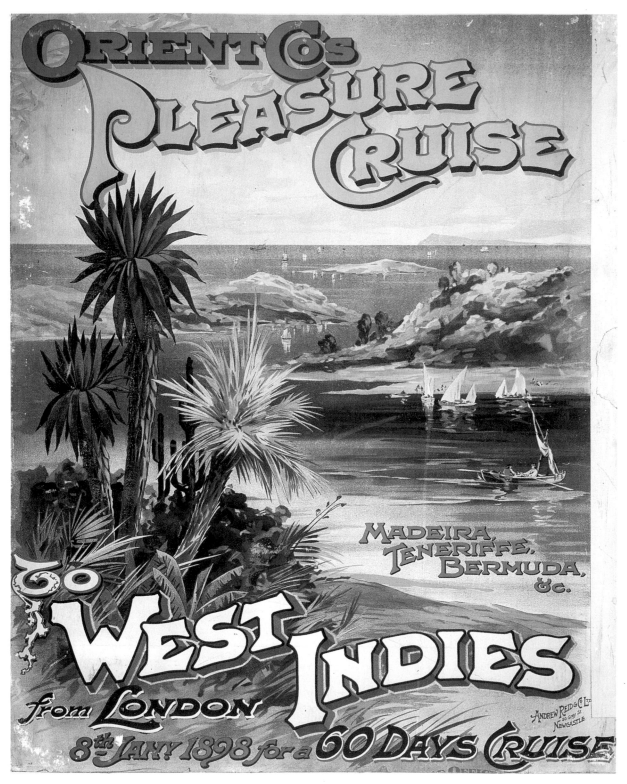

Orient Line cruise poster,
1898; Orient pioneered the
use of surplus ocean liners
for cruising in the 1880s,
sailing to the Norwegian
fiords, the Mediterranean
and the Caribbean – still
popular destinations for
today's cruise passengers.

54

(*Opposite*)
P&O Summer Cruises
brochure cover for 1913.
Cruises seem to have been
more leisurely than today,
and passengers were
prepared to accept delays and
formalities at ports of call
that no modern-day
holidaymakers would
tolerate.

5

CREWS AND PASSENGERS

P&O has always evolved to keep up with the times and to match the evolution of the Empire. It is still doing this now. But it had to persevere with the overland route at Suez for 25 or 30 years from 1843 when the *Hindostan* came into service until 1869 when the Suez Canal was opened – and indeed for some years after that – and in that quarter century, one might say, it evolved its essential quality. Not that it has remained the same since then. Most things in the world have changed since that time, and P&O would not have survived if it had not changed with them.

Everyone on board a P&O ship was aware of that essential quality but it is not easy to put into words. It was a matter of feeling; an atmosphere of pride and self-confidence that ran through the whole organization, an atmosphere that was rare in the early days and is still rare today. One recent commander, retiring in 1953, defined it as 'a reputation for comfortable efficiency ... an individual atmosphere compounded of welcome, warm but not effusive luxury, insidious but never blatant, and a certain distinction, very hard to define, the sort of thing to be found in good hotels or clubs to which wealth alone does not give the entrée. But a hotel never acquires the individuality of a ship; no one ever dreams of talking about a hotel as "her".'

There was no deception about it. The directors in London truly thought a P&O ship was better than any other; they worked very hard to make it so, and they managed to spread the belief to all their crews and shore stations which were soon scattered round the world. Spreading that unquestioning faith began with their careful choice of captains. Most of them were naval. There was a superfluity of naval captains at the time when P&O began, because the Navy had been shrinking since the end of Napoleon's wars. The choice was wide and they found the captains they wanted by paying them very well and showing they trusted them. Trust was all-important then, long before radio, when a captain was entirely alone with his responsibilities.

Junior officers often started very young in the company. In the earliest days, they also joined from the Navy or from other shipping lines, but the company preferred to do its own training, where everyone was taught to live under stern discipline. Long after they were appointed and went to sea, all who had a department to run, the Chief Officers, Chief Engineers and Pursers (and the Captains themselves) were deluged with written instructions, which told them exactly what was expected of them, what they had to expect of their juniors, and especially how they must treat their passengers. Some of these instructions were clearly important, some seem trivial but no officer was left in any doubt of what the company thought he ought to do. Here are a few examples:

(Opposite)
Deck of the P&O steam vessel *Madras* (1,185 tons, built 1852); P&O believed its ships to be better than any others, and the crews also believed this, so passengers soon became aware of 'that essential quality' that meant P&O.
(Watercolour by William Carpenter, 1854)

To Chief Engineers, 1867 : 'Complaints have been made that for some reason there seems to have been a sort of antagonistic feeling between the engineers and (deck) officers which has been very hurtful to the Company's interests.... If such ideas exist, they must be at once abandoned. It is most important that perfect confidence should exist between the engine and deck departments.'

To Commanders : 'We fear there is too much laxity permitted to the officers in associating with the passengers. Courtesy and politeness to passengers are essential, but there is no necessity for carrying this to the point of intimacy.'

To Pursers, 1885 : 'Early tea and coffee.... The bedroom stewards and stewardesses will, of course, attend to those passengers who wish tea or coffee in their cabins. Care must be taken that they are not served cold. The tea should be made in the Rockingham tea pots supplied for the purpose.'

Circular, 1881 : 'It has come to our knowledge that great laxity exists in some of the Company's ships with respect to card playing for money, and gambling in other forms. Such practices are not in accordance with the high state of discipline we expect maintained in the vessels of this Company, and are liable to lead to unpleasant results ...'

To Pursers : 'You must always keep a watchful eye over the stewards and stewardesses.... The Company pays high wages, and have a right to expect the best service. Never, therefore, pass up an act of wilful misconduct, whether it be want of cleanliness or laziness.... Never overlook the slightest appearance of levity on the part of the stewardesses.'

A group of P&O Engineers meeting aboard *Simla* (2,441 tons, built 1854) in 1866 under the leadership of the Company's celebrated Superintendent Engineer Andrew Lamb, in the white top hat.

Chief Engineers seem to have received more of this advice than anyone, but always with the understanding that they had a difficult and dangerous job, and that stokers, especially British ones, were hard to control: 'You must keep a proper subordination by not mixing too freely or familiarly with them, but at the same time you should be careful to avoid harshness or any appearance of overbearing severity.' They must never indulge the inexcusable and filthy practice of lying down on their bunks in their working clothes: 'However tired a man may be, ten minutes can always be spared to clean himself, and his sleep will be thus rendered far more refreshing and beneficial. A bathroom has been specially provided for engineers.' An Engineer Officer should be careful not to 'spend too much of his time in the saloon and on the quarterdeck . . . "Quarterdeck Engineers" are not looked on with favour by the Managing Directors.'

It would not be surprising if officers had resented this stream of advice and admonition, but there is no evidence that they did. Like anyone joining a P&O ship, whether as stoker or commander, passenger or crew, they saw it as a self-conscious and not unfriendly organization, and were glad to be told how they could fit into it, how they could help its smooth efficiency; whatever their job, they learned not only the

Officers and some of the crew of *Benares* in 1862. Asian seamen were recruited as soon as P&O ships sailed in eastern seas, and after the Suez Canal opened spread westwards to the whole of the company's fleet.

59

Bill of Fare aboard *Pera* on 14 September 1859, when she was between Malta and Alexandria on the run from Southampton. The last line is worthy of note.

penalties for doing it badly but the pleasures of doing it well. They knew there were always seamen among the directors – Bourne and Anderson, for example – and they trusted them to know what they were talking about. The directors also had a courteous knack of conveying sympathy even in their rebukes, and they knew the value of what the Navy calls a happy ship. Pride in his ship is always latent in a sailor, waiting to be awakened, and P&O was always good at awakening it.

The company emphasized its difference from others, whether deliberately or not, by using terms of its own. The men who ran it were not a Board of Directors but the Court of Directors. Its captains were always called Commanders. Its shareholders were proprietors, and in addressing them, the Court was punctilious in referring to *your* ships, *your* fleet.

When P&O first started to operate in the East, it had to create a niche for itself among the existing institutions by doing its job better than anyone else. This it did, not only in reliability and punctuality, but above all in building and nurturing corporate pride.

The closest contact between passengers and crews arose, one way and another, from the passengers' food and drink and the care and kindness of the stewards of the Purser's department. Passengers on ocean liners always have incentives to eat too much, unless they are seasick: the cost of the food is included in the price of the ticket, so they have the feeling they have paid for the food whether they eat it or not. P&O was proud of the food it provided, as it was of everything else. 'The intention of the company,' it wrote in one of its circulars to Pursers, 'is that the fare should be plain but of the best quality of its kind, with good, sound wines. The greatest pains are taken by the Company to provide the table in a way that may give general satisfaction, and the prices paid by the Company are liberal.' The food was certainly plentiful, filling and essentially British, except for the company's Indian curries, which were celebrated among connoisseurs. A few menus have been preserved. This one is headed 'P&O *SS Simla*, 15th day of January 1862', an average day on an average ship, between Suez and Ceylon.

Mutton Broth

Roast Turkeys		Boiled Legs Mutton
,,	Sucking Pigs	,,　　Fowls
,,	Fore Qrs Mutton	Fowl & Ham Pies
,,	Geese	Kidney Pudding
,,	Ducks	Sheep's Head Braized
,,	Fowls	Pig's Feet Stewed
,,	Beef	Chicken Sauté
,,	Haunch Mutton	Curry and Rice

Corned Beef

2nd Course

Fruit Tarts	Jam Tartlets
Black Cap Pudding	Sponge Cakes
Sandwich Pastry	Brighton Rocks
Apple Turnovers	Pancakes

Rice Puddings

Now, one might think a diet of so much meat was unhealthy but that was what the British liked to eat in the middle of the nineteenth century, if they could afford it, and the only recorded complaints were made by Australian farmers who thought the food was too 'recherché'. One, after working his way through five or six dishes of meat and more of pastries and cheeses in the heat of the Red Sea, was quoted as saying, 'Well, when I get ashore, I hope I'll find something fit for an Englishman to eat.'

P&O passengers had the same incentive to drink: until the year 1874, wine, beer, spirits and mineral waters were also included in the fares. Unlimited quantities of them were always at hand for passengers to help themselves; which most of them did, beginning the day with claret for breakfast (P&O was famous for its choice of clarets) and steadily progressing towards the brandy and gin at bedtime. On days to be celebrated, Sundays or leaving or approaching harbour, champagne was also free. Some people were undoubtedly more or less drunk all the time but there were seldom complaints of drunkenness. Unless they were abstainers by conviction, the British were heavy drinkers by habit and they were used to it.

Pursers had many difficult jobs. Among everything else, they had to

This 'remarkably select dinner party' on board *Vectis*, Monday 28 November 1853, was adversely affected by the ship's tendency to roll heavily, rather than any shortcomings in P&O cuisine. (This was not P&O's pioneer cruise ship, but an earlier paddle steamer of the same name – see also page 91.)
(Watercolour by E.J.Hall)

P. & O. PENCILLINGS.

1. THE ONLY COOL PLACE IN THE SHIP IS THE REFRIGERATOR, FROM WHICH ON CERTAIN DAYS A STRING OF COOKS AND HELPERS STAGGER BENEATH LOADS OF MEAT FROZEN AS HARD AS IRON, AND DUCKS AND GEESE OF THE CONSISTENCY OF CAST STEEL.

2. WHILE ON SUCH OCCASIONS VISITORS ARE ALLOWED A BRIEF INSPECTION OF THE ICY COLD BLACK HOLE STOCKED WITH MEAT, AND WITH, PERHAPS, A HEAP OF SNOW IN THE CORNER.

3. THE GULF OF SUEZ AND THE RANGE OF JEB EL ATTAKA.

IN THE RED SEA.

In 1890 the artist W.W. Lloyd published his *P&O Pencillings*, a volume of watercolours and pen-and-ink sketches which give a detailed idea of a passenger's experiences *en route* to India. Refrigeration was a quite recent development which had transformed catering arrangements.

do the shopping except when the ships were at home in England, and it was never easy to keep up the continuous supply of food, especially of vast quantities of meat, in ships that had no refrigeration or artificial ice (small and inadequate amounts of natural ice were imported from Canada). The ships left their home port with whole farmyards on board, doomed to be eaten, the birds and animals and the tons of fodder and stacks of hay they needed – not to mention the farmers. Some passengers liked to wake up to the homely sounds of cattle, pigs, sheep, cocks and hens, geese and turkeys. It made a change from the unfamiliar noises of the engine and the sea. But nobody, at such close quarters, enjoyed the smells of the midden and the slaughter house.

Most of this, of course, was for the first-class passengers. There was also a second class, who were fed well but without the lavish choice of the first. In early days, the first class was much the larger of the two, roughly two first-class passengers to one second-class. The poor did not

P. & O. PENCILLINGS.

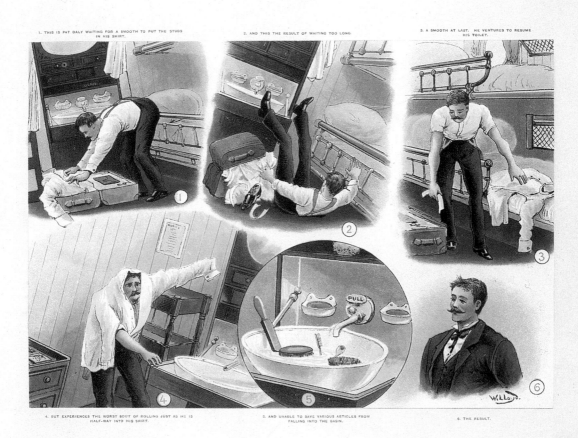

1. THIS IS PAT DALY WAITING FOR A SMOOTH TO PUT THE STUDS IN HIS SHIRT.
2. AND THIS THE RESULT OF WAITING TOO LONG.
3. A SMOOTH AT LAST. HE VENTURES TO RESUME HIS TOILET.
4. BUT EXPERIENCES THE WORST BOUT OF ROLLING JUST AS HE IS HALF-WAY INTO HIS SHIRT.
5. AND UNABLE TO SAVE VARIOUS ARTICLES FROM FALLING INTO THE BASIN.
6. THE RESULT.

IN THE BAY.—DRESSING FOR DINNER.

travel long distances then, unless as emigrants in special emigrant ships. If there was any emigrant traffic to India, it did not go there by P&O, and most of the second-class passengers were the servants the first-class took with them, the batmen of the army officers, the maids of the memsahibs, and the Indian ayahs who looked after their children. Among them were a few people whose pay was notoriously low and whose life was deliberately humble, the clergymen and missionaries.

Many of the passengers wrote letters or diaries – partly perhaps because they did not have much else to do, and partly because the voyage was a rare and novel experience. In the beginning, they wrote mostly about the discomfort, not of the ship itself but of the Biscay gales, the dust and smells of Egypt, and the heat of the Red Sea and the Indian Ocean. As time passed and these troubles to some degree were overcome, they wrote more about the social life on board and the entertainments.

The Bay of Biscay has long held a reputation for rough seas. Aboard ships smaller than today's cross-Channel ferries and without stabilisers, conditions could be very uncomfortable, but social niceties had to be maintained!

The latter seem to have been shared by the first and second class, the concerts and deck games and competitions, even perhaps the dances and fancy-dress balls. So was the Sunday service conducted on deck by the Commander. Most of the entertainments seem dull and even childish but of course all home entertainment then was homemade, and people were accustomed to amateur performers. Thus: 'A gay and festive scene was witnessed on deck or in the saloons at any hour of the day. Deck games and music were in full swing, with an occasional after-dinner dance to the lively accompaniment of the stewards' small but excellent band.' Or again: 'On Thursday and Friday afternoons the various committees appointed were busily engaged in carrying out the sports arranged. Quoits, bull, potato race, egg-and-spoon race, tugs-of-war, skipping contests, thread-needle races, etc., in addition to chess, whist, euchre, cribbage tournaments provided an abundance of amusements.' Or finally, and possibly dullest of all: 'On Tuesday evening a grand concert was given by the passengers of the Second Saloon. The night was warm so the piano was taken on deck and awnings were arranged to make the best of the singing. Mr Rooney opened with a violin selection from Martha, then Mr Pountney rendered "My Sweetheart when a Boy" and Miss Vivian "The Daily Question". Mr Whittaker followed with a recitation capitally rendered, "In the Engine Shed". That fine song "The Mighty Deep" was rendered by Mr Hosking; Miss Davis played "Dans les Bois" as a piano selection, and Dr Smith's burly voice rolled out "Father O'Flynn". Four little maids then concluded the first part by "I don't want to play in your yard". After a brief interval Mr

(*Above*)
'On the way to India – Sunday at Sea.' Passengers aboard *Sumatra* attend Divine Service taken by the Captain, a duty he was obliged to perform by P&O's regulations.
(Engraving from *The Graphic*, 10 April 1875)

(*Opposite*)
Assorted fancy dress displayed aboard *Valetta* in the late 1800s. A similar group forty years later would have appeared little changed in its essentially amateur approach – professional entertainers are largely a postwar development for P&O.

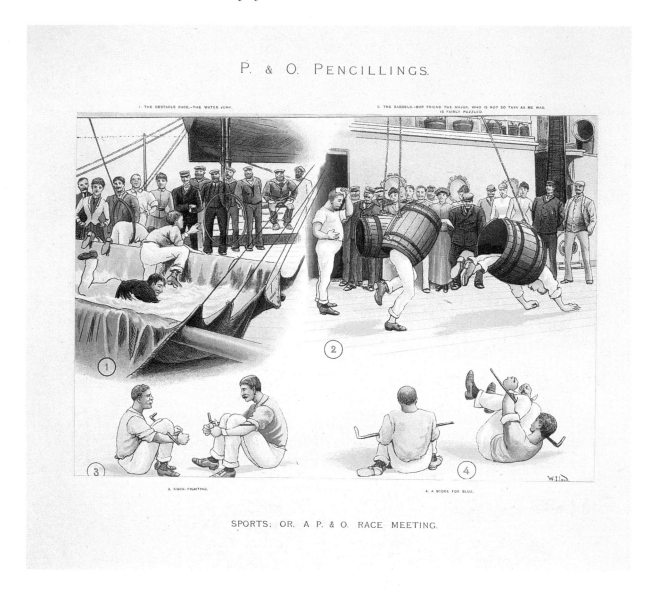

P. & O. PENCILLINGS.

1. THE OBSTACLE RACE.—THE WATER JUMP.

2. THE BARRELS.—OUR FRIEND THE MAJOR, WHO IS NOT SO THIN AS HE WAS, IS FAIRLY PUZZLED.

3. COCK-FIGHTING.

4. A SCORE FOR BLUE.

SPORTS; OR, A P. & O. RACE MEETING.

On a voyage of several weeks, entertainments of all kinds were a must to avoid boredom. Facilities were often rudimentary (sports decks as such were a 1930's innovation) but passengers always managed to enjoy themselves.

Hosking sang "Simon the Cellarer" and encored the last verse. A recitation, "The Elf Child" by little Miss May Longmore was followed by "The Death of Nelson" by Mr Whittaker, who had to respond to an imperative encore, and rendered "'Tis but a little faded flower".'

Perhaps more absorbing than the entertainment was the social life. Each new complement of first-class passengers constructed its own hierarchy, strict and snobbish. There were often two or three generals on board, and many senior administrators or civil servants, and each of them had his own little circle of sycophants and expected his own dignity to be observed. At dinner, these were the people who sat at the commander's table. Much lower down the scale were the young ladies known as the fishing fleet, who were going to India with no other plan but to capture a husband, preferably a rich one, or at least one with prospects for riches. Their flirtations entranced the young men and distressed the older ladies. The slang word 'posh' is said to have had its origin in the snobbishness of P&O passengers, though etymologists deny it. The course on the outward voyage down the Red Sea and across the Indian Ocean was east or southeast, and on the homeward voyage the opposite. Both ways, the cabins on the more northerly side were consequently cooler and people aware of their own importance demanded cabins on the port side outward bound and the starboard side going home: Port Out, Starboard Home. If they got them, their own poshness

1. A distinguished passenger: Gen. Sir F. Roberts.
2. Our Captain, P and O. C° Steamer 'Paramatta'
3. Passengers on the look-out, in the Suez Canal.
4. Afternoon tea-party in the Red Sea.....
5. A perplexed lottery manager.....
6. In the music room...........
7. Summer and Winter......

'Every P&O passenger list is a mosaic of British activities, official and unofficial, in the vast and populous regions of the Eastern Seas.' An assortment of passengers is shown aboard *Parramatta* on the Australian run. (Engraving from *Illustrated London News*, 2 January 1886)

67

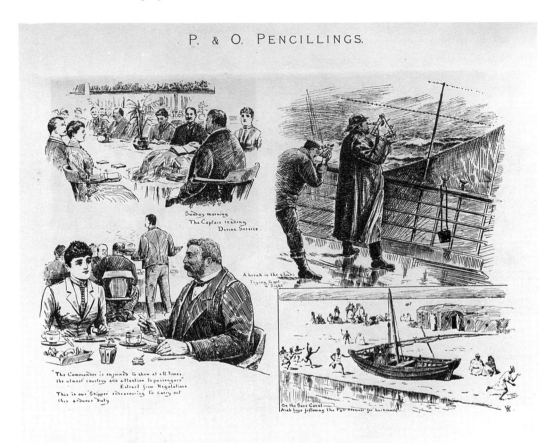

P. & O. PENCILLINGS.

SOME OF THE CAPTAIN'S DUTIES.   ARAB BOYS.

ELEVEN O'CLOCK
BOVRIL

was confirmed. If they demanded them and failed to get them, no doubt they kept quiet about it.

First class on P&O was, therefore, a microcosm of the privileged, esoteric life of British India. For newcomers, it was an introduction to the life they were going to live, and for those who were lucky enough to go home on leave it bought an extra six weeks of holiday. The British loved it and gladly admitted P&O as a part, an important part, of the Raj. In England, India began at Victoria Station or Charing Cross, where the P&O special trains steamed out twice a week for the south. In India if anyone glimpsed the P&O house flag on a ship in port, they recognized the romantic link with home. They were proud of P&O and proud that it was British.

P&O special train at Marseilles: passengers wishing to save time could book a train in London and travel across Europe to pick up their ship at a Mediterranean port. For years this was Marseilles, then Brindisi in Italy, then back to Marseilles at the time of the First World War.

(*Opposite above*)
Navigation was and remains only part of the duties of the Captain of a P&O passenger ship.

(*Opposite below*)
'Eleven O'Clock Bovril' advertisement from a P&O booking office album, *c.*1905. Free liquor had long since disappeared from the Company's ships for economic as well as temperance reasons.

(*Above*)
Before 1854, P&O
passengers to India could
travel by the long route to
Calcutta on the east coast or
wait at Suez or Aden for an
East India Company
connection to Bombay.
When the Bombay route
passed to P&O it gave them a
near-monopoly of steamers
east of Suez, until French
ships such as this one
appeared in the 1860s.
(Watercolour from a
scrapbook by Sir Richard
Strachey, 1866)

(*Right*)
'Group of negro men and
boys taken from a captured
dhow, in a state of
starvation'. The war against
slavery was never-ending.

GROUP OF NEGRO MEN AND BOYS TAKEN OUT OF CAPTURED DHOW IN A STATE OF STARVATION.

6

EASTERN SEAS

Some naive passengers steaming for the first time out of Suez to the south were surprised to find that the Red Sea was not red, but as blue as any other. They knew they were passing close to Mecca and that the barren hills they saw to port were biblical lands long before they were Muslim. But they did not know how ancient their history was or that the Greeks and Romans had used the same word, red, for the whole of the Indian Ocean and the Persian Gulf. According to Persian legend and archeological research, a tribe called the Red Men, or the Men of Erythras, migrated from the land of Elam, which was in Persia, crossed the Gulf, settled on the island of Bahrain and spread from there round the Arabian shore. It was not the sea that was red, but the men who became the first to sail it thousands of years ago.

One measure of the antiquity of eastern navigation is that the first book of sailing directions for the coast of England was written in the fourteenth century, while the first known for the Red Sea was written by a Greek who lived in Alexandria at the time when St Paul was making his voyages, the first century AD.

That wonderful book described the dangers of navigation in the Red Sea and how to avoid them. The west side was friendly enough and had good harbours, but the whole of the Arabian side was dangerous, 'without harbours, with bad anchorages, foul, inaccessible because of breakers and rocks, and terrible in every way.... Those surviving from shipwrecks are taken as slaves.... Therefore we hold our course down the middle of the gulf and pass on as fast as possible.'

That coast was still terrible in 1850 and shipwrecked mariners could still be taken as slaves. Nobody seems to have told the passengers of P&O but its ships still held a course down the middle and passed on as fast as possible until they came to Aden.

Aden by then was a British colony and P&O had a major coaling station there. The place was extremely hot and entirely barren and few people wanted to go ashore. This was where the annoying gap began in the P&O domain. Its ships could not go on to Bombay, the nearest port in India, because the East India Company still claimed a monopoly of that route. Passengers in a desperate hurry to reach Bombay had to make a choice: either to wait in the inhospitable dust and desert of Aden until an East India Company ship came in, or to go on to Madras, Calcutta and the east coast of India by P&O. Unless they had recently passed one of the rival ships coming down the Red Sea, most preferred to stay on board where they were and go the long way round.

The same book of first-century sailing directions described how the courses diverged and how Arab navigators followed them, steering by the monsoon wind and checking their course and latitude, 1,000 years before the compass, from the direction and elevation of the Pole Star. 'Those bound for Damirica (roughly where P&O were bound) set their ship's head considerably off the wind; while those bound for Barygaza (which was near Bombay) keep along shore for not more than three days, then hold the same course out to sea with a favourable wind, quite away from the land.' The ships of 1850, of course, had the compass but they may have found the steady wind and the stars were as good or even better guides.

Aden in 1850 was still a centre of the long frustrating struggle of the Royal Navy against the slave trade from East Africa to Arabia. Passengers must have seen the frigates, wearing the White Ensign, which were always gathered there, and no doubt their senior officers came aboard the liners for a drink and a good meal. Indeed, one captain, named Colomb, came out as a passenger with P&O to join his ship *HMS Dryad*. But probably as loyal officers they did not talk about their troubles.

The British aversion to slavery was based in the awful cruelties of the trade on the other side of Africa and across the Atlantic to America. The Arabian trade was very different. Its cruelties were in the villages where Arabs captured Africans and on the long marches in chains to the coast.

The naval frigates pursued any Arab dhows which looked as if they might have slaves among the miscellaneous cargo they carried from Africa to Arabia. Frigates were the fastest ships of the Navy but in a good wind they could not overhaul a good dhow. Some of them had auxiliary engines by then but coal was rare and expensive, and they did not get up steam until they sighted a likely dhow; for if one of them chased a dhow which turned out to have no slaves on board, the Admiralty expected the captain to pay for the coal he had wasted. If they did find slaves, they found they did not want to be rescued and were ready to swear they had been born in Arabia – for they were treated on board with the casual kindness of any passenger in a dhow, and by then they had met the ex-slaves in the crew who told them of the possible pleasures of life in Arabia, and also that the British were cannibals who only wanted to capture them for a feast. The British captains knew that if they did catch a dhow and liberate some slaves, they had nothing to offer them that was much better than slavery. It was out of the question to land them again in Africa; they would never have found their way home, they would either have starved or been captured and sold again. So they took them to Aden where they were confined in huts on an island. When a shipload had been collected they were sent to Bombay, a totally foreign land from which they could never hope to return, where they kept themselves just alive with jobs that the lowest caste of Indians would not or could not do. The English captains, all facing an early death from the dysentery and malaria of East African swamps, came to believe they were fighting the wrong people in the wrong place, antagonizing the Arab skippers they liked and admired, and doing no good to anyone.

The P&O officers knew they were passing through this melancholy battlefield, where the British Navy for once was engaged in a fight it could never win. But there is no reason to think that most of the

passengers knew it. The ships ploughed on through it all in the scarcely bearable heat until at last Ceylon was sighted, which seemed to the passengers, after Egypt and Aden, to be an earthly paradise.

That difficult and illogical ban on the Bombay route, with the awkward trans-shipment of passengers and their baggage from one line to the other at Aden, lasted for ten years after P&O was established east of Suez. But in the meantime, P&O was thinking of venturing farther east, and to that end it was busily building more ships. The growth in the number and size of its ships is still remarkable. In 1840, when it took on the Alexandria route, it could claim to have seven. In 1850 it had 23, five years later it had 42, and by 1867 it had 51. As the ships grew bigger and bigger, the figure of its total tonnage climbed even more steeply: 6,500 tons in 1840 to 85,000 tons in 1867.

The growth was the more remarkable because the design and building of steamships was evolving all the time: iron was replacing wood, the screw propeller was replacing paddles and steam engines themselves were changing from simple, to compound and then to triple expansion. All these innovations led to greater efficiency in miles per ton of coal, so they could not be neglected, and though P&O seldom actually pioneered technical developments, it always looked at new ideas and techniques to see whether they suited its needs – greater speed, reliability, and improved economy.

The port of Galle, Ceylon, must have seemed to passengers like an 'earthly paradise' after the heat and barrenness of Egypt, the Red Sea and Aden. P&O moved its services to Colombo in 1882.
(Watercolour by A. Nicholl)

73

The first iron ship, for example, is usually thought to have been the *Aaron Manby*, which was built in a Staffordshire ironworks in 1820, taken to London overland in sections, put together on the Thames and used on the direct run from London to Paris up the Seine. (One of the people who put money into building her and lost it was the same Sir Charles Napier – Mad Charlie – whom Anderson met in Portugal.) But P&O did not go into iron (except in the tug *Atfeh*) until 1843, when they launched a steamer of 548 tons which they named *Pacha*, as a compliment to the ruler of Egypt.

It was the same with the screw propeller. The invention of it, by several rivals at the same time, may be dated 1838. P&O built its first propeller-driven ship 13 years later. The compound engine took even longer, 36 years from the first experiments in America in 1824, which were not a success. The whole of that delay was not due to P&O's caution. The new engine was a complicated idea: the exhaust steam from a small high-pressure cylinder was used again in a larger cylinder at lower pressure. It needed a high-pressure boiler to begin with, and though iron-boiler technology improved tremendously between 1840 and 1880, the introduction of steel was to make the higher pressures involved in compound engines easier to maintain.

P&O's hesitation was not timidity. Anderson, and probably others of the Court of Directors, kept a careful eye on new developments, and must have longed now and then to build a really experimental ship. But the company's strength was that Anderson's practical genius was always balanced by Willcox's watchful bookkeeping. If Anderson's ideas ran too far ahead of reality, there was always Willcox to bring them down to earth, and Willcox would certainly have said that experimentation was not the company's job. Its job was solely to build reliable and comfortable ships and run them to the satisfaction of its passengers. That was what it was uniquely good at.

Inevitably, its success brought it enemies. Its growth, especially the growth from seven to 42 ships in the 15 years from 1840 to 1855, came at a time when other shipping lines in both the West and East were failing, falling into bankruptcy or driven to rash actions to avoid it. Naturally, those that knew they were failing were jealous of the one they could see was succeeding. There may have been more personal jealousies too. The officers and shore staff of P&O knew they had the best and most enviable jobs in the shipping world; they may have been boastful and they may have looked down their noses at the officers and staff of lesser companies. P&O was, therefore, accused of having the faults of a monopoly and of making excessive profits.

It was not at all repentant. It did not deny it had won a position of near-monopoly but it absolutely denied it had made an improper use of its success. The moment when a unique success becomes a dangerous monopoly is a matter of opinion. P&O was always able to argue that its strength had been won by sound commercial practice, and that strength had made it able to offer better terms than anyone else for its mail contracts. If this was monopoly, it was a great saving to the tax-payer.

As for its profits, they had been large ever since it began, but this also, it claimed, was through sound financial judgment. Its dividends had

(*Opposite above*) *Nyanza* (2,082 tons, built 1864) was the last paddle steamer built for P&O; naval architecture was moving on and the screw had largely replaced paddles but the older system still found favour on some routes where speed and shallow draught were prerequisites.

(*Opposite below*) Iron hulls gave the rigidity that the long propellor shaft of a screw steamer needed, yet the first seagoing P&O screw steamer, the 546-ton *Shanghai*, was not built until 1851, nine years after their first iron ship, for conservative rather than technical reasons.

risen year by year from $3\frac{1}{2}$ per cent to 8 per cent. Beyond that, further profits were ploughed back by setting up internal Depreciation and Insurance Funds, through which it could survive the risks of the sea and face the occasional losses of ships without a financial strain. A shipping line was a high-risk business and needed a high rate of dividends.

P&O had fewer of those losses than other lines, perhaps through its careful choice of Commanders, but it did not escape them: seafaring then was much more dangerous than it is now, with modern aids to navigation and pilotage. Strangely, P&O's most conspicuous disasters were in European waters, though those were far better charted and lit than the Eastern seas. Year after year, the Court of Directors had no losses to report to the proprietors, but in 1846 it recorded 'with great regret' that the *Great Liverpool*, the first of the two large ships the company had bought for the Alexandria service, had been wrecked off Cape Finisterre.

That was as strange a mishap as the loss of the *Don Juan* nine years before. Finisterre was a passage as well known as any in the world. The ship was northbound: she had come up the coast of Portugal and western Spain. The weather was not particularly bad and the Commander should have known their exact position. It looks as though he, like the Commander of the *Don Juan*, cut his corner and altered course to starboard too soon. She had several hundred people on board. It was said she hit a reef seven miles out from the coast but there is no reef anything like that distance off Finisterre. Whatever she hit, she came off it, but she was badly holed and sinking, and had to be beached on the mainland. The crew got everyone off except three passengers – one woman, a baby and its Indian nurse.

They got the mails off too. The Fourth Officer, whose name was William Bencraft, was a very adventurous man who often shone in a crisis, and when the tide ebbed and left the ship lying on the beach, he cut a hole in her side, hauled out the boxes of mail, loaded them into a local brig and sailed it into Corunna Bay, where he found another P&O ship which could take them on.

The story is incomplete. There is no convincing explanation of why it happened, and no explanation at all of how such a crowd of hundreds was housed and fed in that distant corner of Spain, or of how the passengers were taken home. But the directors' report had a reassuring and rather complacent end. The ship was a total loss but she was insured for two-thirds of her value and was well in credit on her depreciation account. The directors, therefore, felt that 'in a pecuniary point of view, the company did not sustain any loss'. They gave William Bencraft a sextant with a gold arc, and he deserved it. Sadly, and to everyone's regret, Captain McLeod committed suicide.

In its ventures to the Far East, P&O met more dangers: not jealous financiers, but incomplete charts, unpredicted typhoons, well-armed pirates, and the secret wars and workings of the opium trade. And it had to contend with these alone because it had reached the very frontiers of the Empire, and even by its own ships support from home was three months away.

Its first Far Eastern route was comparatively safe and well known:

(*Opposite*)
A sextant presented to Captain T.S.Angus of *China* 'in recollection of many sights and a very pleasant voyage' in 1902.

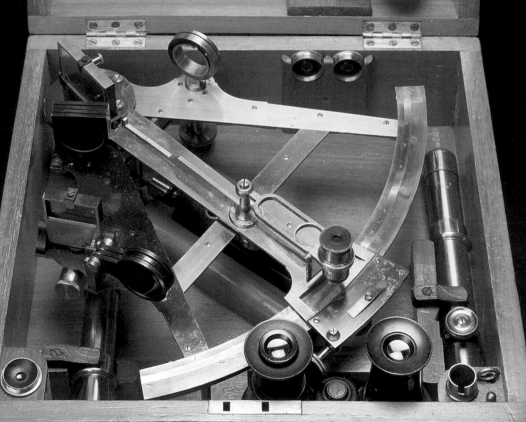

Lady Mary Wood (533 tons, built 1842) began her career on the Peninsula run but in 1845 opened P&O's Far Eastern service, running from Point de Galle via Singapore to Hong Kong. Lady Mary Wood herself was the wife of Charles Wood, Secretary to the Admiralty, later Lord Halifax.
(Zinc engraving by W. A. Delamotte)

from Ceylon or Calcutta through the Strait of Malacca to Penang and Singapore, and thence through the China Sea to Hong Kong. Singapore had been a British colony since 1826 and Hong Kong since 1841. All that time, they had been run like the early Spanish, Dutch and Portuguese colonies in the Spice Islands. That is to say, by a visiting season once a year, when the monsoon allowed it. On 4 August 1845 the first P&O steamer was sighted from Singapore, splashing its way down the Strait: the little *Lady Mary Wood*, 41 days out from London and bringing a promise of regular monthly mails. That promise transformed every institution of the Colony, and of Hong Kong when she got there: their trade, their social and family life, their knowledge of what was happening in the rest of the world, even the type of people who settled there; for most people who had come before had come in the expectation of staying there all their lives, but now there were transient visitors who came one month and might be gone the next.

For that run, P&O had a mail contract which was practically an extension of monopoly. But it needed further use for its growing fleet, and it decided to bring steam to the trade with China, which was mainly a matter of taking silk out and opium in. The silk trade was the most ancient and romantic of Far Eastern trades: the silk had come by the Silk Road, the longest road in the world, from Peking to Constantinople, untold centuries before the time of Marco Polo. The opium trade was comparatively new, and in a modern view it was immoral, for its success depended on making the Chinese a race of drug addicts.

It would be foolish to pretend P&O did not take part in the opium trade. It did. It did not buy or sell opium or anything else: carrying was its job, not trading. The drug was grown in India and the Middle East, but there was a bottomless market for it in China, and there was good freightage to be earned in taking it there. The stuff came into P&O's warehouses packed in crates which were then delivered to China. Of course, P&O knew perfectly well what was inside them but they would have said that was no concern of theirs. The trade was not illegal and nobody then – or nobody that mattered – had thought of it as immoral or seriously worried about its effect on the Chinese. However, in trying to enter that trade, P&O earned the enmity of owners of the fast sailing ships, the opium clippers, who had been running it for years, and stirred up a hornet's nest for themselves.

P&O started sending small steamers on a freight run from Hong Kong to Macao, an old-established trading centre, then up-river to Canton. Another service was opened along the coast to Shanghai. They had no mail contracts beyond Hong Kong but in this case they hoped it would be an advantage to trade wherever there were cargoes, without being tied to a mail delivery.

It was not a success. P&O was too law-abiding and the carriers of drugs too ruthless. P&O was accused of being late with the mails because its ships were overloaded : the bunkers of one were said to be so full of crates of opium that her coal was loaded on deck. It sounds unlikely. But another ship – the *Lady Mary Wood* – was accused of

Capture of Keang-Foo by the British during the Opium Wars of 1839–42. The treaty of Nanking which ended the war ceded Hong Kong to Great Britain and opened up the five 'treaty ports' of Canton, Amoy, Foochow, Ningpo and Shanghai.

P&O's 349-ton steamer *Canton*, built for the Hong Kong/Canton river service in 1848, towing the sailing frigate *HMS Columbine* into action against pirate junks in September 1849.
(Oil by Norman Wilkinson, *c*.1938)

carrying a cargo of silk which had been smuggled through the customs at Shanghai. That story is more plausible: it was a common practice to bribe the Chinese customs rather than pay the duty. P&O insisted the silk had been 'planted' on them but the ship was fined and banned from Canton. That time, P&O took their protest all the way to the Foreign Office in London, and the fine was cancelled, but by the time the decision came back, the *Lady Mary Wood* had lost most of a year's trading and the company had withdrawn her.

The ship *Canton* had one notable success, but a success without any profit. The China Sea was another area where the Royal Navy was active – not against slavers but against pirates in junks. The *Canton* came up with a naval frigate, *HMS Columbine*, in action against a pirate fleet, all under sail. She had already been hit by gun-fire, the wind was falling and the junks were drawing way with oars. The *Canton* passed a rope to the *Columbine* and towed her back into action. The junks were defeated and the *Canton* took the *Columbine*'s wounded back to Hong Kong, earning the Navy's thanks but not much else.

In those distant seas, so far from home, the ships continued to meet adventures, and sometimes disasters. The iron-built *Pacha* collided with another of the company's ships in the Strait of Malacca. She sank abruptly. The *Canton*, after her success with the pirates, hit an uncharted rock in the Canton River and lay there, badly holed and exposed to the weather, for eight weeks before P&O got her off and took her back to Hong Kong. Then three ships left Hong Kong simultaneously. The barometer gave no warning but a very violent typhoon blew up: one of the three survived but two disappeared and were never seen again – and one of them, the 610-ton *Corea*, belonged to P&O. Another typhoon disabled the new steamer *Douro*. She drifted out of control and grounded on the desolate islands of Paracel, 200 miles from anywhere in the South China Sea. Two officers patched up a boat and sailed it to Hong Kong for help, over 400 miles away: a famous small-boat voyage even in those days of sail.

While those salt-sea adventures were happening at the easternmost end of the steamer routes, an extraordinary series of arguments was being fought out at home in both Houses of Parliament. This seems to have been a renewal of the previous attack on P&O, and what started it again seems to have been discussion of plans for a mail service to

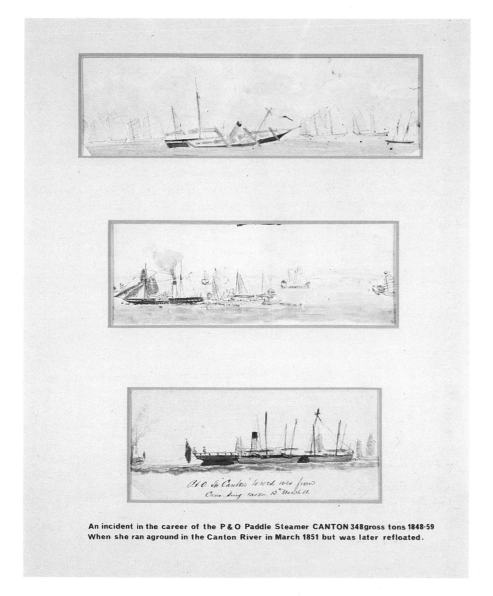

An incident in the career of the P & O Paddle Steamer CANTON 348gross tons 1848-59 When she ran aground in the Canton River in March 1851 but was later refloated.

Canton ran aground on an uncharted rock in the Canton River in March 1851, and remained stuck for eight weeks before being refloated and repaired – an admirable advertisement for iron ships.

Australia. Of course, there was room for discussion, simply because there were so many possible routes to Australia: round the Cape of Good Hope, round Cape Horn, across the Isthmus of Panama, by way of San Francisco, or by a branch at Ceylon or Singapore from P&O's eastern route. It was complicated because the separate colonial governments of Australia could not agree among themselves. New South Wales wanted a service to Sydney from San Francisco, Western Australia wanted it from Singapore to Perth or Albany, and South Australia between the two insisted on a terminus at Adelaide. A route from Singapore to Sydney via the Torres Strait was also proposed, and another from Aden to Albany with a coaling station in Mauritius. Commercially, the whole thing was dubious because of the vast distances and the unanswerable questions of how many people might use the service if it existed. P&O made at least four suggestions and even offered to run the route and share any profits or losses with the home and colonial governments. But while that offer was 'on the table', the Government offered a charter of incorporation and a contract to another company, almost unknown, which proved to have no ships that could do the job. It offered to sell its charter to P&O, attempted to run the service, and then went bankrupt.

Looking back at that stupendous argument over a century later, one is inclined to think that P&O must have been at fault somewhere, that there could not have been quite so much smoke without fire. But however hard one searches, one cannot find that the company did anything a company should not have done. It was always perfectly open in its dealings with the Government. Accused of making excessive profits, it invited the Government to inspect its meticulous accounts, which it did. Accused of running its schedules late, it published figures which proved its astonishing punctuality. There were always those who

For steamers, you had to have coal. That was difficult and dirty enough. Then you had to have stokers, frequently 'seedies' from East Africa, and the 'stokehole' where they had to work was indescribable. (Watercolour from *P&O Pencillings* by W.W.Lloyd, 1890)

tried to find fault with its ships, or its crews, or its elaborate organization, or its treatment of its staff, but P&O seems to have made its main enemies solely by being too successful.

Perhaps the most difficult part of the argument was to persuade its critics how much more there was in running a good steamer line beyond just providing the steamers. For one thing, there was the coal. There had been no coal east of Suez until P&O took it there, and every ton of it still had to be carried by sailing ships round the Cape, or past Suez by camels. At a time when the company was running 50 steamers it needed 170 sailing colliers, chartered from other companies, to keep its stocks of coal up to the 90,000 tons it thought was a safe minimum, in 14 coaling stations. And food: P&O fed 10,000 people every day, in 50 floating hotels which were always on the move. In places like Suez, there was only suitable food because P&O owned and ran farms to produce it, and there was no drinking water. All these things had to be provided in the right quantities at the right places and times, nearly half-way round the world.

One has to simplify, if not over-simplify, the arguments which went on, not only in Parliament and many boardrooms, but also, no doubt, over dinner tables and privately over port. Both Anderson and Willcox were Members of Parliament at that time, and Anderson in particular, as Radical member for Orkney and Shetland, was known as a 'bonny fighter', a forceful speaker in debate, with a style all his own. He found himself defending P&O until every one of its established routes was under question – not only its routes beyond Suez but its contract for the route to Alexandria, almost its first, was due for renewal and was under attack. Indeed, the last ship under the original Indian contract had sailed before the Government made up its mind how to run the route in the future. For a while, the whole great organization that Anderson and his colleagues had created seemed to depend on his single voice in debate.

The opposition was defeated quite suddenly. What seems to have happened was that P&O made yet another offer to solve the Australian problem. It suggested a service from Bombay to the Australian ports. That meant it also had to offer, yet again, to take over the route from Suez to Bombay. That route, in the hands of the East India Company, was disliked by its passengers and was known to be costing the governments of Britain and India between them £105,000 a year. P&O was able to offer to do it for £24,700, and to use much better ships for the purpose. That was a difference nobody could logically refuse, and it is said the East India Company put the lid on it by losing a complete consignment of mail. They found they had no ship to take it from Aden to Bombay, so they loaded it in an Arab dhow which left port and was not seen again. There may also have been another final straw. P&O was so much faster and more reliable, combined with the development of Indian railways, that it was almost quicker to send a letter from England, addressed to Bombay, by way of Calcutta.

Towards the end of the 1850s, the arguments died away. Rivals gave up attacking P&O, at least for the present, and one by one all the eastern steamer routes fell back into its hands, just because nobody else could

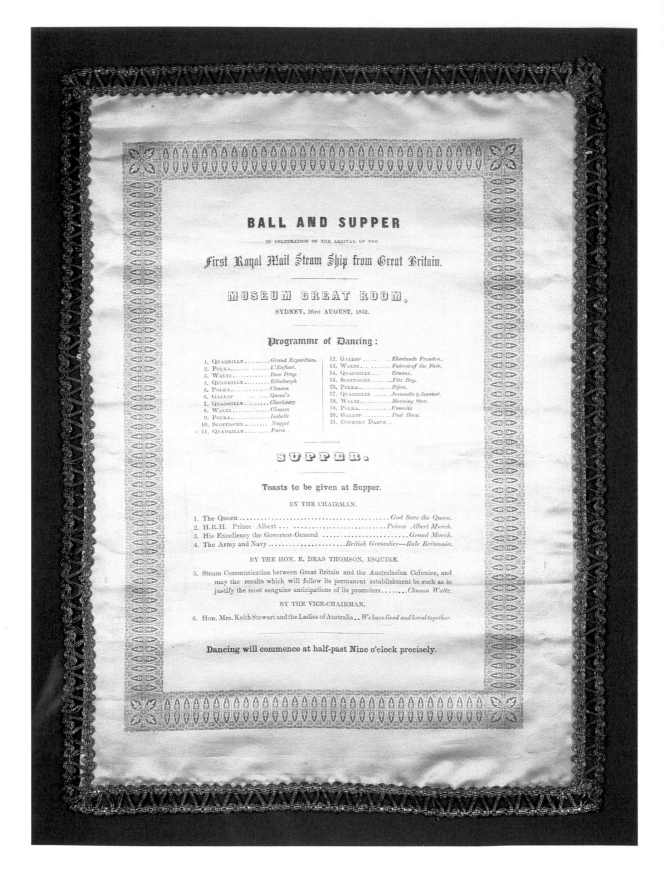

run them so cheaply and efficiently: England to Bombay, Ceylon, Calcutta; on to Singapore, Hong Kong and Australia; and even a new extension to Japan. A historian of the company 30 years later could write that P&O was 'in possession of all the lines of steam communication between England and the Far East – a position which had assuredly not been attained through official favour or influence, but for which the managers of the undertaking had fought many a stout fight, cheered, no doubt, by the confidence of their Shareholders, and the consciousness of pursuing a straightforward and honourable policy.'

But it could not last. Three more menaces were looming. One was a substantial rise in the cost of coal; another was the Crimean War; and the third and worst was the opening of the Suez Canal.

(Opposite and below) In the 1840s P&O made several proposals for mail services between Britain and Australia. None was immediately taken up, but in the end a contract between Sydney and Singapore was granted, and the arrival of the 699-ton *Chusan* to open the service was joyously celebrated in Australia. There was even a waltz composed to mark the occasion.

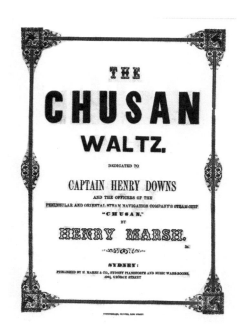

THE

CHUSAN

WALTZ.

DEDICATED TO

CAPTAIN HENRY DOWNS

AND THE OFFICERS OF THE

PENINSULAR AND ORIENTAL STEAM NAVIGATION COMPANY'S STEAM-SHIP

"CHUSAN,"

BY

HENRY MARSH.

SYDNEY:

PUBLISHED BY H. MARSH & CO., SYDNEY PIANOFORTE AND MUSIC WARE-ROOMS, 404½, GEORGE STREET

7

THE CRIMEAN WAR
AND THE CANAL

These menaces fell upon P&O at a difficult time, when its founders were simultaneously growing old. Captain Richard Bourne was the first of them to die, in 1851. His part in the beginning remains rather enigmatic, but he was the original man of experience who had come to know and trust the other two, Willcox and Anderson. He had apparently taught them how to raise capital and had certainly chartered them their earliest ships. In the first directors' report after his death, they referred to his energetic and enterprising spirit, and gave him most of the credit for founding the Incorporated Company. But they also referred to his impaired health, and it seems that failing health, as his old age approached, put an end to his activity and made people look on him as a source of solid wisdom which had faded.

Next, in 1854, Willcox resigned as Managing Director, after making over most of his income to the company which had paid it. However, he remained a member of the Court of Directors and indeed became Chairman in 1858, holding that post until he was killed by a falling tree in 1862. That unusual accident must have upset the unique balance of daring and caution which had been the company's strength for so long, the balance of Anderson's daring and Willcox's caution.

(*Far left*)
The Crimean War is remembered, among other things, for Florence Nightingale and the Charge of the Light Brigade. The services rendered to the Allied forces by merchant shipping companies, however ill-managed the military campaign, have received less recognition than they justly deserve.
(*Print by R. Caton Woodville, 1895*)

(*Left*)
Arthur Anderson aboard one of his own steam yachts towards the end of his life.

Anderson did not retire. He was already Managing Director and succeeded Willcox as Chairman; he remained Chairman until he died in 1868, at the age of 76. He was still full of energy but he applied a lot of it to philanthropy and to enjoying a series of large steam yachts. Like Willcox, he gave much of his income back to the company, in order to found a 'provident and good service fund' for the company's staff. He had started his career without a penny to buy a piece of bread but he ended it a rich and well-known benefactor. In Southampton, which had become the company's home port, he founded a school for 800 of the children of the staff. At his home in Norwood, south of London, he endowed a Working Man's Institute. In his native Shetland Islands he built and endowed a home for the widows of fishermen, in memory of his wife, and a school which is now the secondary school for the Islands is still known by his name. He also pestered the Government for a steam mail service to replace an ancient one under sail, and he founded a Shetland Fishery Company in competition with the archaic and ungenerous system of landlords' fishing tenures under which the local people laboured.

It is only a guess that these interests took a lot of his time from P&O, and that there was a noticeable weakening in the company's direction. But it is a fact, to be seen with hindsight, that things began to go wrong.

The shortage and cost of coal was a problem the directors could not completely solve. They did what they could about it, investigating the idea of getting coal from mines in Borneo, but this was expensive, and there was also a shortage of sailing ships to bring the coal so far. They had to buy two colliers to help in fetching it and that put the price up further. But with enough forethought they could perhaps have avoided being stuck, as they were, with new contracts which had eight years to run, at the very moment when the cost of coal was about to rise by 50 per cent.

They made another mistake, which they soon had to admit: they built a ship almost twice the size of any they had built before. This was the *Himalaya*, 3,500 tons, 340 feet long, with engines sometimes described as 700 horsepower and sometimes as 2,000. She cost about £130,000, and was said in turn to be the biggest ship in the world. But measurements of ships were vague, and if she was bigger than Brunel's *Great Britain*, which had been in service for most of 10 years it was only by a few feet; and she was hardly half the size of his *Great Eastern*, which was already on the stocks.

It seemed to everyone just then that ships would go on being bigger and bigger for ever. So they did, of course; but it was a process that had to have pauses while other techniques caught up with the mere mechanics of building hulls, and this was one of the moments when a pause was needed. Sheer size, without more complex engines, was a cul-de-sac in ship design in the 1850s. P&O took the wrong turning.

They were not the only company to make this mistake; Brunel did the same. The mistake was a hangover from the battle Brunel and others had waged against the calculations of the Rev. Dr Lardner some 20 years before. It still seemed that the range of a steamer depended on its size: the bigger it was, the further it could steam without coaling.

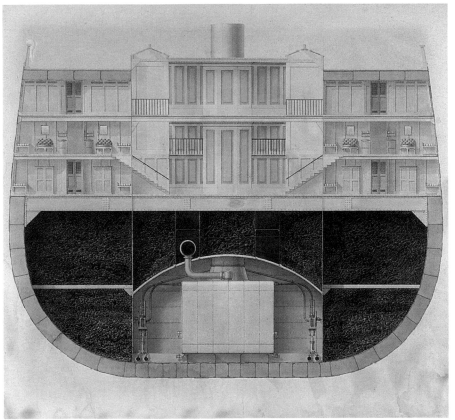

(*Above*) P&O's first *Himalaya*, completed at the end of 1853, was at 3,438 tons half as big again as any ship the company had built before. She proved too expensive to run and was sold to the Government as a troopship, where her size was of more importance than her profligacy with coal. (Unsigned oil *c.*1949 after lithograph by T.G.Dutton)

(*Left*) Brunel's 18,915-ton *Great Eastern*, finished in 1859, was designed for direct voyages to India or Australia without refuelling, but proved too large and expensive for commercial service. She was five times the tonnage of the largest P&O ship when she was completed, and larger than any of the company's ships built until 1923.

Probably P&O was attracted by the idea of fewer and more convenient coaling stations. Brunel was also looking towards the East. His *Great Eastern* was designed for the run to Ceylon. In theory, she could have steamed from England to Ceylon and back round the Cape, carrying 15,000 tons of coal and 4,500 passengers, and it was thought Ceylon would become a point of assembly for passengers all over the East. P&O never owned her, nor probably wanted to – luckily, for the pursuit of size was a fallacy. There was another way of increasing a steamer's range: to improve the efficiency of its boilers and engine. This was on the verge of being achieved, with the screw propeller and the compound engine. The *Himalaya* was half-way to achieving it, but only half-way. She was laid down as a paddle steamer and altered, like the *Great Britain*, to screw propulsion while she was being built. But she still had a 'simple' type two-cylinder engine with pistons 7 feet in diameter and 3½ feet in stroke. Consequently, she still consumed a prodigious amount of coal. She was too expensive to run and lost money on every trip. Brunel died of a stroke two days before the maiden voyage of his final dinosaur and did not see her failure; P&O's mistake had been made before the death of Willcox, so he and Anderson had to find a way out of it.

There was another interruption in P&O's shipbuilding programme at about the same time, when the Admiralty suddenly said it objected to mails being carried in iron ships. Even P&O, never an innovator, had been building iron ships since 1842, and carrying the mail in them. Iron had been proved through long experience to be safer and better than wood. The Admiralty's whimsical objection was that they could patch a shot-hole in a wooden hull but had no way of doing it in iron. Nobody could imagine circumstances in which a ship would be shot at when it had mails on board. But as ever, the Admiralty's arguments avoided logic, which made them hard to answer, and for a while the directors had to contemplate reviving old-fashioned wooden ships to carry the mails, while using the newer iron ones to carry the passengers. They talked the Admiralty out of it in the end but it took time.

Then came the Crimean War, from 1854 to 1856. That was the first war, at least since the seventeenth century, which had much direct effect on merchant shipping; for in the Napoleonic wars, the Royal Navy had been huge and quite capable of the duties of a navy without the help of merchant ships. The Crimean War was different. The Navy had degenerated. Most major warships were still under sail, and through its rigid system of promotion all its senior officers were old men. When the war began, Lieutenants could be in their sixties. The Navy's Commander-in-Chief (C-in-C) Plymouth was 81; the C-in-C West Indies was 79, and applied for the more active war command of the Baltic. But that was given to Mad Charlie Napier who was 68, while the Black Sea, the most active of all, went to Sir James Dundas, who was 69. However, the most immediate need was transporting very large armies and their horses and equipment to distant battlefields. That was largely the Army's concern, and the Army, for all its famous shortcomings in that war, had none of the Navy's prejudice against steamships. As ever, it did not like going to sea, but if it had to be done it preferred to do so

PENINSULAR & ORIENTAL STEAM NAVIGATION COMPANY'S SHIP
VECTIS

under steam. It did it very largely in P&O's ships; the company had carried troops on and off since 1840, and by 1855, 11 of its best and biggest ships, a third of their total tonnage, were working in the Black Sea, taking troops to the Crimea and bringing back wounded to the notorious hospitals at Scutari. It is said they carried in all 2,000 officers, 60,000 men and 15,000 horses, not to mention guns, ammunition and all sorts of stores.

It was this war, some 40 years after the advent of steam at sea, that put an end at last to the Navy's dislike of it. Even though it had 200 steam warships of all classes and there were no unpowered ships in the Baltic Fleet, the pace of change had been slow. Without any question the presence of P&O ships in the zone of battle helped to speed the change: its large ships, confident and efficient, managed things the Navy could not possibly have done under sail. There was practically no fighting at sea but many duels between ships and shore batteries; steamers were able to keep out of trouble while sailing ships would have been caught at a hopeless disadvantage. Best of all, they could go close in to the enemy shore, land their troops and go astern to get out again.

Of course, it was out of the question suddenly to transform the Navy from sail to steam. But in the Crimea, the Admiralty suddenly changed its intentions: it decided to create a steam fighting fleet as quickly as it could. It started in a very practical way with the new concept of the steam gunboat. Gunboats could be built quickly and cheaply, even in those days, by a kind of mass production. The idea was to build the smallest possible ships with the biggest possible guns, and a standard gunboat was 100–120 feet in length overall, with an engine of 20–60 horsepower and – in the early days – a full rig of sail too. Each of them carried a 68-pounder forward, a 32-pounder aft, and two 24-pounders amidships.

There was no room for naval pomp in such very small ships. They had so little room below that it was said tall officers had to shave with their heads sticking out of a skylight and the mirror propped on deck. Yet they brought back pride to the Navy and a new efficiency. For 40-odd years young men had had no chance of command, they could only wait for older men to die. Gunboats gave them a chance and they made the most of it: each one was commanded by a young man, usually in his twenties. Nearly 200 of them were built and commissioned in 1855 and 1856, and they were still being built at the end of the nineteenth century. If P&O could be said to have been the Empire's postman, gunboats were the equivalent of the policeman on his beat. They could and did turn up anywhere in the world where there was trouble, burning coal if they could get it and wood if they could not. They seldom had to fire their monster guns. In those days, the sight of a ship with the White Ensign, however small, steaming into a roadstead or a river mouth with a conscious air of nonchalant rectitude, was enough to discourage most troublemakers, such as Arab slavers or Chinese pirates. The old naval officers, who had been so scornful of steam, had to admit it needed uncommon skill to navigate these clumsy little steamers around the world; and for the young men who did it, it was the life of adventure they had hoped for when they joined the Navy.

P&O had, therefore, played a large part in bringing steam to the Navy

GOING TO THE WAR.
No. 4.
EMBARKATION OF THE 93rd HIGHLANDERS AT PLYMOUTH, MARCH 1st 1854, IN THE GREAT STEAM SHIP "HIMALAYA."

READ & Co., 10, JOHNSON'S COURT, FLEET STREET.

and might have been proud of what it did; but at first, as ship after ship was swallowed up by Government service, it showed no signs of pride but only of irritation at the disruption of its ordinary services. Many of its regular lines had to be cut down, made monthly instead of fortnightly, and a few, particularly the new Australian service, had to be abandoned altogether while the war lasted. It must indeed have been annoying to have to stop the work the company had existed for, the things it did so well. But it cannot be said it suffered financially. The Government paid reasonable rates for the ships on war service. Among other things, it bought the *Himalaya*. She made a splendid troopship. Refitted for trooping, enormous numbers of men, guns and horses could be crammed into her, and the directors persuaded the Government to pay £133,000 for her, which was just about what she cost. So the company found its way out of that mistake, and the Government got a bargain. She remained a troop ship for 30 years, and might have had as long a life as her contemporary the *Great Britain*, but that while she was still afloat as a coal hulk in World War II, she was hit by a German bomb and sank in Weymouth harbour.

P&O's irritation at the disruption of war was understandable. It was used to making good profits by doing things particularly well. In war service, it made a bare living by just existing, and there was no pleasure or satisfaction in that. It was not until the war was over that it began to

Embarkation of the 93rd Highlanders in *Himalaya* at Plymouth, 1 March 1854. After one commercial voyage to Alexandria, she was chartered for Crimean trooping and then sold to the Government in July 1854.

93

understand that just by existing it had done a patriotic duty nobody else could have done. Without its great reserve of reliable steamships and its special knowledge, could the Crimean War have ever been won, or a few years later, the Indian mutiny defeated?

However, the next challenge to P&O came from a totally unexpected and contrary direction: a revival in sailing ships. It was strange that sailing ships only reached their ultimate grandeur after they were obsolete; strange also that their revival was an offshoot of steam. But so it was. What happened was that engineers began to apply their science to the design of hulls. They began with steamer hulls, doing their best to make them easier to drive, and so to achieve a little more speed, range and economy. But most of the calculations they made were valid for sailing hulls too; new sailing ships began to appear with finer lines than any had had before, and a ratio of beam to length that had not been seen since the Viking ships or the medieval fighting galleys of the Mediterranean. In the cult of the clipper, sail plans and rigging were elaborated until a crack sailing ship could set 30 square sails and 15 fore-and-afters, and such a ship in a fair wind could be faster than any steamship of the time. On the other hand, with a contrary wind or no wind at all, she was obviously slower. Fast sailing became a mixture of sport and commerce. Rival nations ran races to Australia and the East and back again.

Many such ships were built in Britain, but this was something Americans excelled in, and for a while New England ships could beat all

The tea clippers *Ariel* and *Taeping* approaching London at the end of their 16,000-mile, 99-day race from Foochow in 1866, which saw them and the *Serica* docking within two hours of each other, and two other ships two days later. (Lithograph by T.G.Dutton)

Mooltan, built
in 1861, introduced
compound engines to the
P&O fleet. Fuel consumption
figures were halved.
(Lithograph by
T. G. Dutton)

comers on the long sea-routes. The most publicized of all the races were in the tea trade, to be the first to reach England with the new season's China tea. They began as an Anglo-American competition but when the Americans' interest began to wane at the time of the Civil War, the British ships fought against each other. The most memorable race was in 1866, when three ships left port in China on the same day. They separated, and did not sight each other until they were in the approaches to the English Channel. The race was won by ten minutes in a voyage of 99 days. But that was not a record time. The American *Witch of the Wave* set a record of 90 days in 1852, and the British did not beat it until *Sir Lancelot* took a day off it in 1869.

Many people, including P&O, tried to rationalize this competition. It was obvious that the fastest of all would be a first-class sailing ship with an auxiliary engine to help it through the calms. P&O started to design such a ship. For a line which had been founded entirely on steam, that could only have been a step backwards; luckily they decided to try a compound engine first. In 1861 they came up with the *Mooltan* of 2,257 tons, with screw propulsion and a complex type of engine which halved the normal coal consumption and solved that problem once and for all.

It was doubly fortunate they decided to stick to steam; for 1869, the year when *Sir Lancelot* set her record, was also the year when the Suez Canal was opened. That was the beginning of the end of sailing ships.

The opening of the Canal was also nearly the end of P&O. Looking back with a superficial glance, one would have thought the Canal would have solved the worst of the company's troubles by cutting through the barrier which had always divided its fleet and its operations into two. But it was not so simple. For several years it brought more problems than it solved.

Very unluckily, Arthur Anderson, with his genius for problems, died the year before the Canal was opened, and the new set of problems was left to his successors, of whom the young Thomas Sutherland soon came to the fore. Sutherland, one must say at once, was extremely

Ferdinand de Lesseps and his Suez Canal. P&O (and British opinion generally) doubted whether the project would be a success. They could not have been more wrong!
(Cartoon from *Le Hanneton*, 12 September 1867)

Opening of the Suez Canal by Empress Eugénie of France on 17 November 1869. P&O's *Delta* carried Government representatives half way through the new waterway, but British reaction continued to be lukewarm.

competent but it was hard for him to have such tests at the very beginning of his reign.

The new problems were not technical but political, and the fundamental cause of them was that P&O, the leading shipping line, was British but the Canal was French. Nobody in Britain thought the French would ever succeed in building the Canal. The official opinion of the British Government was expressed by Lord Palmerston, who said a canal was a physical impossibility, that if it were built it would injure British maritime supremacy, and that 'the proposal was merely a device for French interference in the East'. This rather pig-headed opinion had its origin nearly 50 years before, at the time when Napoleon conquered Egypt and planned a canal that was part of his scheme to 'interfere in the East'. That scheme was thwarted by Nelson in the Battle of the Nile but, almost a lifetime later, the British Government was still suspicious that the French were up to their tricks again.

Perhaps P&O should have known better. Its own employees could watch what was going on between Suez and the Mediterranean. In the past, it had often disagreed with the Post Office or the Admiralty, and said so, and been right. But now it was up against the Foreign Office; its headquarters were not, after all, in Egypt but in the City of London so it could hardly be blamed if it followed the official view.

However, the Foreign Office was mistaken. It had not understood the peculiarly French genius of Ferdinand de Lesseps, and his fanatical, patriotic and passionate faith. It assumed de Lesseps was only an engineer. If he had been, he might have had to listen to the predictions of failure that came from all sides, but he was not. He was a French consular official who had been posted to Cairo in 1833, and his interest in canals was historical rather than technical. He had read and been told that early Egyptians had dug out canals in various periods which joined the Red Sea to the Nile and his unshakeable belief was that anything early Egyptians could do could be done again by French engineers in the 19th century. Anyone who disagreed was lacking not only in knowledge but in faith.

It took him a very long time to collect the huge sums of money he needed, but once that was done the work went ahead surprisingly quickly, partly done by masses of forced labourers who dug, like the ancients, with their hands, and latterly by mechanical dredgers which were only slightly less primitive. De Lesseps gave the first ceremonial 'blow of the pickaxe' at the Mediterranean end in 1859, and ten years later the first ceremonial convoy passed through from one end to the other. One P&O ship, the wooden paddle steamer *Delta*, joined the procession, carrying three P&O directors, but only went half-way through and then turned back. In the following month, the directors' report said: 'The proprietors may feel assured that whenever it may be for the advantage of the company to make use of it [the canal] the opportunity will not be neglected.'

That report looks complacent. The Canal existed, P&O's rivals were queuing to use it and yet P&O appeared to be in no particular hurry. They were not the only people who remained somewhat unenthusiastic about the Canal even after it was officially opened, for its finances were still precarious, it tottered for several years on the edge of bankruptcy, and engineers said that desert winds would fill it with sand again. It has been said that P&O was so sure the Canal would be abandoned and everything would go back to normal that they built 23 new ships in the ten years while de Lesseps was at work, and that at least five were too deep in draft to go through. That may not have been strictly true. But what was true (and the directors confessed it) was that after the Canal was ready, P&O had to 'sell at a sacrifice about 40,000 tons of their older vessels, most of which, except that they could not carry sufficient cargo, were fit for several years work; and at the same time it was necessary to build upwards of 80,000 tons of new ships'.

The key to this statement was that the ships could not carry sufficient cargo. All kinds of owners had been building freighters since the Canal even looked as if it might be ready – ships far cheaper to build and run than the company's liners – and P&O found they were seriously losing trade. The company had always made its income from passengers' fares, the mail contracts, and freight on small amounts of valuable cargoes, especially silks and what was called specie – in other words, gold and silver coinage. The newcomers proved they could undercut its rates for freight. There were two reasons: one that its fast mail ships were always expensive, and the other, that after all its years of pioneering it was left with overheads far higher than anyone else. All over the East it had had

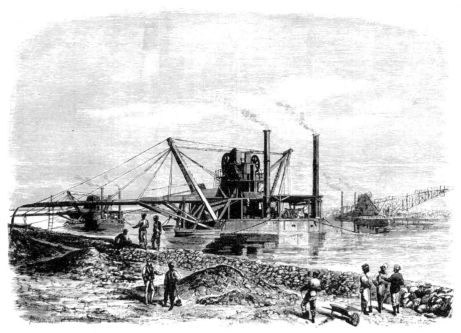

THE ISTHMUS OF SUEZ MARITIME CANAL: DREDGES AND ELEVATORS AT WORK.

(*Left*)
Dredgers and elevators at work digging the Suez Canal. Machinery was introduced when the Egyptian authorities imposed a reduction on the number of manual labourers permitted to work on the project. (Engraving from *Illustrated London News*, 3 April 1869)

(*Below*)
P&O had to build new ships suitable for the changed trading conditions brought about by the Suez Canal. One of the first, the 3,900-ton *Peshawur*, was completed in 1871. Here she passes one of the ubiquitous dredgers.

to build itself offices, dockyards and repair shops which were essential when it started but useless and unsaleable when the Canal made it cheaper to send ships home for refits and repairs.

P&O had spent very extensively in Egypt: the docks, warehouses, lighters and coal dumps at Alexandria and Suez; hotels at Suez and Cairo; a large share of the railway which it had financed for the Pasha; fruit, vegetable and sheep farms to feed the passengers; steamers on the Nile, roads, vehicles, camels; and ships' stores which were said to stock everything from needles to anchors. Even the lighthouses down the Red Sea, which everyone used, had been sited, built and manned by P&O.

So it saw two alternatives: either to join the ranks of companies running cheap freighters, or to take as little notice as possible of the Canal, rebuild its fleet to the highest possible standard, and then in its own time hope to establish again the supreme position it had held for so long. It chose the second.

There was yet another reason why it had to scrap so many ships and build so many new ones. That was the new compound engine which was

In time P&O used the Suez Canal enthusiastically, and it was the Post Office which had to be converted. Here one of the Jubilee class of 1887 8 enters the Canal at Port Said, southward bound with the mails.
(Watercolour from *P&O Pencillings* by W.W.Lloyd, 1890)

P. & O. PENCILLINGS.

OUTWARD BOUND P. & O. MAIL STEAMER ENTERING THE SUEZ CANAL.

PORT SAID.

so much more economical that nobody could afford to be without it. What with the loss of freight, the dead weight of the overheads and the expense of new ships, P&O, a couple of years after the Canal was opened, found its income was regularly falling by £100,000 a year, and it could not pay a dividend. The Post Office chose that delicate moment for a sly move of its own. The old mail contract, which had several more years to run, said the mails must be carried overland past Suez: when the contract was drafted there was no other way they could go. P&O now wanted to send ships through the Canal for the sake of its passengers and it naturally wanted to send mails in them. The Post Office imagined P&O was trying to reduce its costs, and refused to let the company do as it wished, unless it would accept a reduction of £30,000 a year in its mail subsidy. The old contract said the mails must go overland and that was that.

In fact, it made little difference to the cost whichever way the mails went. P&O, whose ships were entrusted with the mail the remainder of the way to the Far East and back, wanted the same ships to take them the last 100 miles through the Canal. It was only common sense. They saw no reason why they should pay tens of thousands of pounds for the privilege.

At last, the two great institutions came to a ludicrous compromise that had no common sense at all. P&O began to land the mails at Alexandria or Suez, send the ships through the Canal, send the mails by the old route overland, and then pick up the same mails with the same ships at the other end. That fulfilled the letter of the law and allowed it to draw its full subsidy. It made the Post Office even angrier but they could not legally stop it, and this ludicrous arrangement went on for two years before a more sensible plan was agreed.

8

PAX BRITANNICA

All these political battles had to be fought by Thomas Sutherland. He had joined the company as some sort of office boy in London when he was 18, and when he was 20 it sent him East, first to Bombay and then straight on to the very end of the line at Hong Kong. He was Anderson's own choice as a future Chairman but he was not the immediate successor. Two others held the post between Anderson's death and Sutherland's appointment, but neither made much impression.

It is not impossible that Anderson knew Sutherland previously, but as it happens the young Aberdonian got his job through James Allan, the other Managing Director and a family friend, while he was only moved from Bombay to the Far East because Henry Bayley, one of the senior managers, wanted to make space for an acquaintance. This however put him where he could make his mark, and he stayed in Hong Kong for twelve years with everything he did closely watched by the Court of Directors far away in London.

It was a continuous success story. Hong Kong in those days was not a comfortable place to live. It was even unhealthier than Egypt and was also the sort of place where everyone slept with a revolver under his pillow – there was a price on the head of every European. Few people endured it more than a year or two, but Sutherland survived, permanently full of energy and enterprise, to become the company's senior man and, therefore, a leading figure in the community. He was

Thomas Sutherland (centre) with P&O colleagues at Hong Kong. A contemporary wrote, 'We have few men with better heads and more enlightened and refined ideas than Sutherland has.'

The P&O office opened at no. 14, Yamashita-cho, Naka-ku in Yokohama in 1866. On a private visit Sutherland had got agreement to run a regular mail service to Japan, and P&O sailings had begun in 1859.
(Dyed silk by Kunitsuru, 1866)

popular both among the British and the Chinese, which was an unusual feat; 'a little king in Hong Kong', somebody wrote, 'and all over China'. His juniors liked him too. People competed for jobs under Sutherland, who they said was 'a good businessman and a gentleman: you always knew where you were with him'.

It seems that the Japanese felt the same. He took a lift in a sailing ship in 1859 to Nagasaki, where half a dozen Dutchman were the only foreigners who had permits to trade. He was only there a week but he came away with an oral agreement for a regular steam mail service, the first of its kind to join the secretive people of Japan to the outside world.

He was brought back to London with a large reputation when he was 32. That was in 1866, with P&O on the brink of a financial crisis. Before he died Anderson may well have instigated Sutherland's becoming Assistant Manager, and in 1872 when he was still in his thirties the rest of the Court appointed him Managing Director. He was very young for the post but nobody knew more about P&O; so he was the man who had to do battle with the Post Office, rebuild the fleet and cut down the expensive possessions overseas.

The last of these three jobs was perhaps the most delicate. During a phase of the Industrial Revolution when managers were often ruthless, P&O had always been unusual in valuing the loyalty of its staff. That may have been Anderson's influence; he was certainly kind and sympathetic, and there is no reason to think the other founders were less so. Or it may have been simply that they knew a loyal staff was good for their particularly widespread trade. Anyhow, Sutherland was evidently of the same mind. He managed to streamline the staff without undermining its loyalty, and at the end of it all the company was more economical and efficient.

He was right too in deciding not to go in for cheap freighters but to keep up the company's standard by building only high-quality mail steamers, but building them faster and bigger than they had been before – faster to fulfil more demanding mail schedules, and bigger, so that they had space for more mundane cargoes and were not confined to silk and specie. In 1870, the year after the Canal opened, P&O's fleet was

down to 44 ships with an average tonnage of 1,857; by the year 1884 it had grown to 50 ships of about twice the average size – and the Canal had been dredged and widened to take them. The company had not only recovered from its Suez crisis: it was stronger and greater than ever.

There were still problems to come and changes to be faced. This was bound to happen in a trade that evolved so quickly. Probably the biggest change was the development of the electric telegraph from the middle of the nineteenth century.

That did not only affect P&O. It brought into existence a whole new kind of maritime trade: tramp steamers. Not everyone knows the difference exactly between a liner and a tramp. It is not just a matter of size or ornament or comfort or even speed, though P&O looked down on what they called 'a cheap class of cargo boats'. The real difference was in how they were organized. A liner had to run always on the same course or line – hence its name; it could not deviate because it had to run to a timetable, especially if it was under a mail contract. A tramp on the other hand was ordered by its owners to any port which was known to have a cargo for it, and that was why tramp steamers only came into existence when the electric telegraph made possible a worldwide system of cables to inform the owners where the cargoes were and to order the ships to go there. Tramps could always offer lower freight rates than liners, while liners offered regularity, speed and a chance of planning ahead for months or even years. Tramp trade was seasonal: if a rice crop failed in Burma, say, the ships could be diverted to carry Australian grain, while liners had to go to their advertised ports whether cargoes or passengers were awaiting them or not. That was an added reason why P&O lost trade with the opening of the Suez Canal: the Canal happened to coincide with the invention of the telegraph. It was a pressure P&O had to submit to. Sutherland's solution was to build or buy a few of the despised class of steamers, but to put them on branch lines and use them in coordination with the liners. So they succeeded to some extent in combining the regularity of the liners with the elasticity of the tramps, bringing the liner service to minor ports and bringing more regular cargoes and passengers into the centres where the liners could pick them up. It was a compromise, but it worked. P&O remained the luxury service it had always been, but some time in the 1890s its receipts from freight caught up with and passed its receipts from passengers.

Indirectly, the growing financial importance of freight led Sutherland to decide the home port in England had to be moved from Southampton to London. Most passengers preferred Southampton, which saved them at least a day at sea, but shippers would not pay extra for the carriage of their goods by rail, and using Southampton was losing the company trade. That was another move which meant an upheaval of employees who had lived most of their lives in Southampton and had sent their children to the company school that Anderson had founded. For many families it must have been a traumatic upset and there is no record of how it was achieved.

All this time, argument about the Suez Canal rumbled on in London, even after Disraeli's dramatic purchase of Canal company shares. That purchase gave the British places on the Canal company's Board of

(Opposite above) The 1870s saw a great increase in the P&O fleet. The new ships were conventional and comfortable, carried more cargo than before, and were good revenue-earners. The 3,536-ton *Nepaul* built in 1876 was a handsome example.

(Opposite below) While P&O concentrated on the prestige mail services, other owners were introducing steam to lesser trades. *Trewidden* was built in 1878 as the first tramp steamer of the celebrated Hain Steamship Company, later a P&O subsidiary.

Directors but it still seemed to them that the French were using the Canal as a weapon against them – not particularly against P&O but against all British ships. The French had set up a Sanitary Board in Egypt, nominally meant to keep the country free of cholera. It decreed that if a ship passed through the Canal without a clean bill of health, it must not have any contact with the shore, and nobody on shore must go on board it. Yet all ships using the Canal had to be controlled by a pilot. In effect, no ship – and they were mostly British – which approached from the south could present a bill of health from every Eastern port she had called at, some of which might have had a case of cholera. British ships were told that they must have a pilot, that he must not go on the ship but go ahead of it in a tug boat, shouting his instructions. That took an unconscionable time, the Canal company charged the earth for it, and it led to frequent strandings.

The French would have taken a different view and insisted their Sanitary Board was a necessary protection. But it never got to that stage. The British Foreign Office, still hating the thought that the Canal was under French control, demanded a second canal, to be strictly British, and in 1883 it offered de Lesseps £8 million to dig it.

Sutherland was elected Chairman of a Committee representing all the British shipping lines which used or might use the Canal, with instructions to put the scheme into effect. De Lesseps had all the cards in his hand, not least the firm offer of £8 million. But luckily Sutherland, and presumably de Lesseps too, came to see after very long discussions that there must be some more practical answer to the problems, and the rather crazy idea of a second Suez Canal parallel with the first was allowed to fall out of sight.

PUNCH, OR THE LONDON CHARIVARI.—FEBRUARY 26, 1876.

THE LION'S SHARE.
"GARE À QUI LA TOUCHE!"

In November 1875 Disraeli bought Khedive Ismael's shares in the Suez Canal Company. This made Britain the largest single shareholder – hence the title of Tenniel's cartoon.
(*Punch*, 26 February 1876)

P&O's Head Office at 122 Leadenhall Street in the City of London in April 1891. The company had been at this address since 1847, progressively acquiring neighbouring property to extend its premises, and remained in residence until 1964, after which a new P&O Building was erected on the same site.

However, under Sutherland's leadership in those last decades of Pax Britannica, P&O had a period of comparative calm, and this might probably be said to have been the apex of its grandeur, stability and prestige. The British Empire seemd to be eternal and the stream of passengers from Britain to India and back seemed also likely to last for ever. The ships grew in size, in numbers, in speed and in comfort, all with triple-expansion engines and screw propellers, all passing through the Canal and gradually reducing the journey from London to Bombay to 15 days. There were losses, dramas and tragedies at sea but they were part of the nature of a shipping line; and considering that P&O's fleet was steaming $2\frac{1}{2}$ million miles a year, they were remarkably few.

The ships in that era changed completely in outward appearance. Engines and propellers were becoming so safe that auxiliary sails and their rigging could be abandoned; and with them the last vestiges of sailing-ship design, the bowsprits, figureheads and graceful clipper stems began to disappear in the 1870s. P&O did not find it necessary

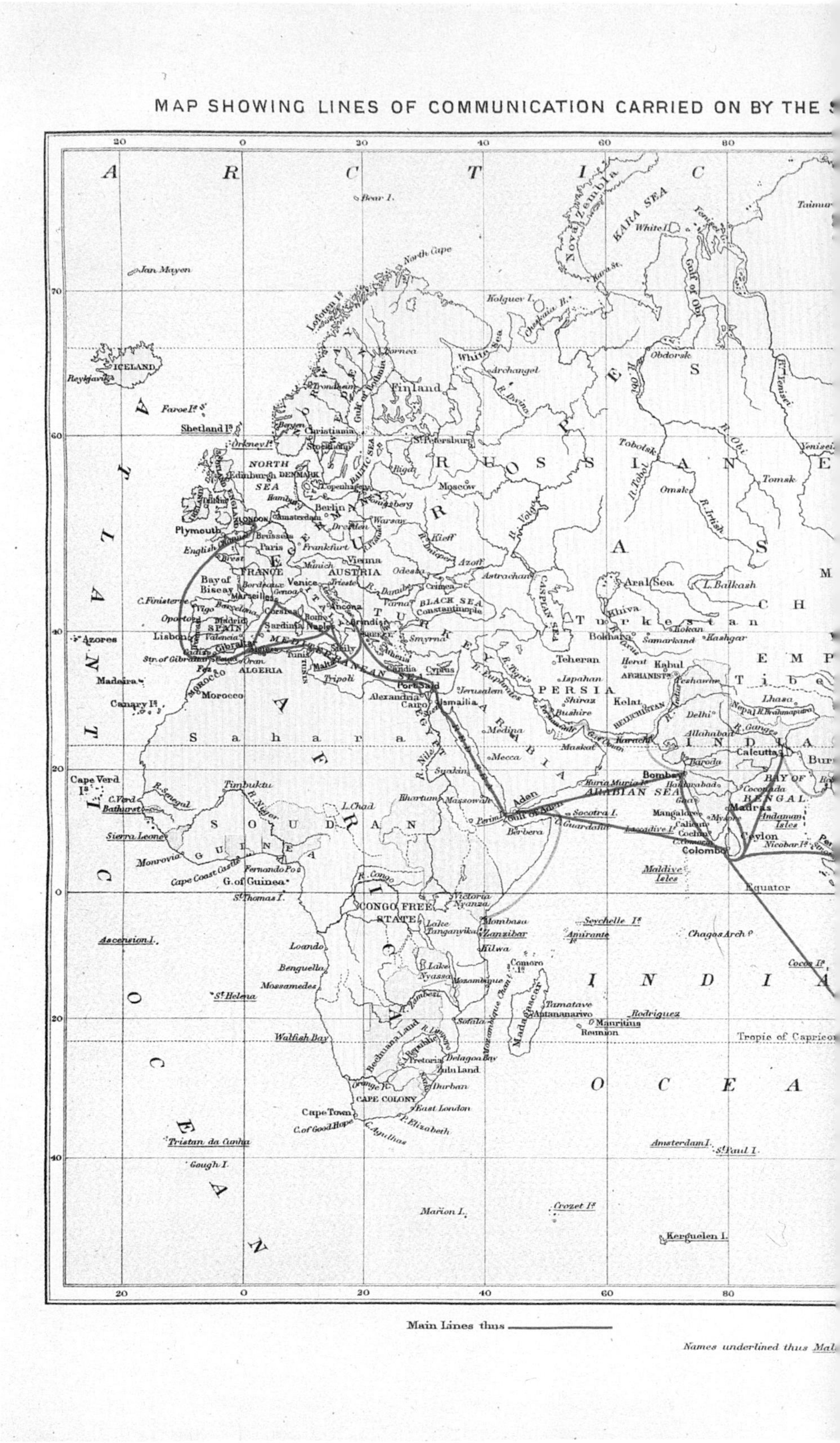

MAP SHOWING LINES OF COMMUNICATION CARRIED ON BY THE S
A R C T I C
A T L A N T I C O C E A N
I N D I A N O C E A N
R U S S I A N E M P
C H I N E S E M P
Bear I.
Jan Mayen
North Cape
Nova Zembla
KARA SEA
White I.
Kolguev I.
White Sea
Archangel
Obdorsk
Gulf of Obi
Tobolsk
Omsk
Tomsk
ICELAND
Reykjavik
Faroe Is.
Shetland Is.
Orkney Is.
NORTH SEA
Edinburgh
DENMARK
Copenhagen
Christiania
Stockholm
St. Petersburg
Riga
Moscow
Finland
Plymouth
LONDON
Amsterdam
Berlin
Warsaw
Kieff
Brussels
Paris
Frankfurt
Vienna
AUSTRIA
Munich
FRANCE
Bay of Biscay
Bordeaux
Marseilles
Genoa
Venice
Trieste
Odessa
Crimea
BLACK SEA
Constantinople
Azoff
Astrachan
CASPIAN SEA
Aral Sea
L. Balkash
C. Finisterre
Vigo
Oporto
Madrid
SPAIN
Lisbon
Barcelona
Corsica
Sardinia
Rome
Naples
Brindisi
Smyrna
Sicily
Malta
Tunis
Tripoli
Candia
Cyprus
Gibraltar
Str. of Gibraltar
Oran
ALGERIA
Fez
MOROCCO
Morocco
Azores
Madeira
Canary Is.
Port Said
Alexandria
Cairo
Ismailia
Jerusalem
Teheran
Ispahan
PERSIA
Shiraz
Bushire
Khiva
Bokhara
Samarkand
Kokan
Kashgar
Herat
Kabul
AFGHANISTAN
Peshawar
BELUCHISTAN
Karachi
Maskat
Delhi
Lhasa
Allahabad
INDIA
Calcutta
Baroda
Bombay
Hyderabad
Goa
Mangalore
Mysore
Madras
Calicut
Cochin
Ceylon
Colombo
Andaman Isles
Nicobar Is.
BAY OF BENGAL
ARABIAN SEA
Kuria Muria Is.
Aden
Gulf of Aden
Perim
Socotra I.
C. Guardafui
Berbera
Laccadive Is.
Maldive Isles
Medina
Mecca
Suakim
Khartum
Massowah
Sahara
SOUDAN
Timbuktu
R. Niger
R. Senegal
L. Chad
Cape Verd Is.
C. Verd
Bathurst
Sierra Leone
Monrovia
GUINEA
Cape Coast Castle
Fernando Po
G. of Guinea
St. Thomas I.
R. Congo
CONGO FREE STATE
Victoria Nyanza
Lake Tanganyika
Mombasa
Zanzibar
Kilwa
Seychelle Is.
Amirante Is.
Chagos Arch.
Equator
Ascension I.
Loanda
Benguella
Mossamedes
St. Helena
Lake Nyassa
Mozambique
Comoro Is.
Madagascar
Tamatave
Antananarivo
Mauritius
Reunion
Rodriguez
Sofala
Walfish Bay
Bechuana Land
Pretoria
Delagoa Bay
Zulu Land
Durban
CAPE COLONY
East London
P. Elizabeth
Cape Town
C. of Good Hope
C. Agulhas
Tristan da Cunha
Gough I.
Amsterdam I.
St. Paul I.
Marion I.
Crozet Is.
Kerguelen I.
Cocos Is.
Tropic of Capricorn
20
0
20
40
60
80
Main Lines thus
Names underlined thus Mal

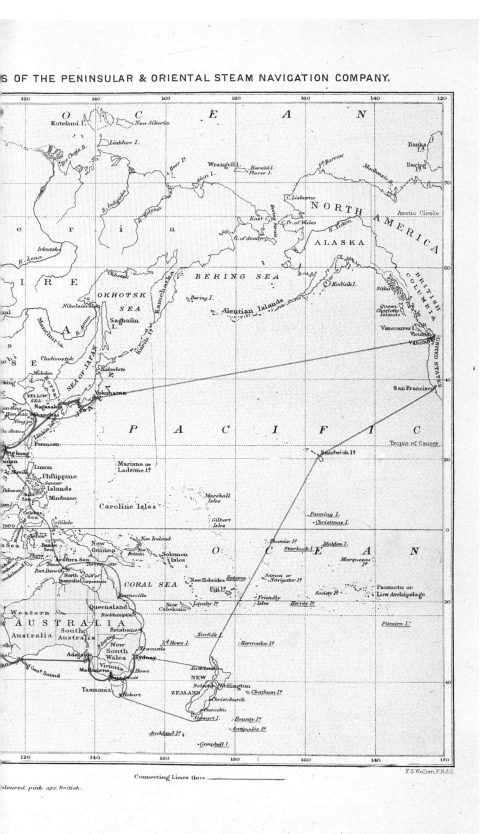

P&O's routes in 1890.
(Map from *P&O Pencillings*
by W.W. Lloyd)

Britannia (6,525 tons, built 1887) was second of the celebrated four-strong 'Jubilee' class. Here she is seen coaling at night in the outer harbour at Aden, a messy job only superseded when P&O converted its passenger fleet to oil fuel in the 1920s.
(Oil by W. Ayers-Ingram)

(*Right*)
Britannia overhauling the sailing ship *Cutty Sark* while both were on the Australian run: the P&O liner on the crack mail service, the clipper carrying wool, very much a comedown from her tea racing days.
(Oil by David Cobb)

(*Opposite*)
Commonwealth (6,612 tons, built 1902) was one of the five-strong Blue Anchor Line fleet which gave P&O a foothold in Australian emigrant traffic via the Cape, a route which it had previously attempted once or twice without success.
(Watercolour by W. Blanchard, 1912)

until 1903 to add to the safety and reliability of its mail steamers by the use of twin screws. Steamers developed a shape and ultimately an elegance and beauty of their own, with straight stems and usually with counter sterns that owed nothing, or nothing visible, to sailing-ship design.

In 1887 the company celebrated its Jubilee, which was also that of Queen Victoria, by building four ships, each over 6,500 tons, and 1,500 tons bigger than any it had built before. And they gave them patriotic names: *Victoria*, *Britannia*, *Oceana* and *Arcadia*.

The most drastic development P&O completed in that era was the take-over of the Blue Anchor Line in 1910. That well-known line, which belonged to the family of Wilhelm Lund, existed mainly to run between Britain and Australia by the Cape, taking emigrants and general cargo out and, at first, bringing China tea and, later, Australian wool on the homeward voyage.

P&O had thought for years of entering the emigrant trade, though it was a wholly different class of shipping from the luxurious mail ships. The difference showed in the accommodation. P&O's first-class passengers were twice as many as the second or tourist class. Blue Anchor steamers on the other hand carried roughly 90 first-class to 450 third-class. It also showed in the appearance of the ships. P&O's were always designed to look elegant, Blue Anchor's even at that time were thought ugly, with hardly any sheer on the hulls and massive masts and funnels set vertically. Nevertheless, they offered a reliable and economical service for emigrants, and did not pretend to compete with the luxurious service by way of Suez. Not even their names were attractive to many people: mainly, they were aboriginal Australian.

However, in 1909 Blue Anchor's largest and newest ship vanished:

Queen Victoria, the Prince of Wales and their party outside the P&O pavilion at the Royal Naval Exhibition in Chelsea in 1891. The company's status as a linchpin of Imperial communications was by now well established.

the *Waratah* of 9,339 tons. She was homeward bound on her second voyage, called for coal at Durban, passed on the next day the *SS Clan MacIntyre*, which was also bound for Capetown, and was never seen again. There was no wreckage, no sign of her 17 lifeboats or of her three rafts, or the bodies of any of the 211 people aboard her. Nothing was washed ashore. The *Clan MacIntyre* reported heavy weather but she and other ships came safely through it. What happened to the *Waratah* remains a mystery of the sea.

That disaster seems to have dispirited the Lund family. The Blue Anchor Line never recovered and six months later P&O was able to buy its assets, business and goodwill for £275,000. The name of Blue Anchor disappeared. It became the P&O Branch Line, and with that P&O entered both extremes of the passenger trade, the first-class service by Suez and the cheapest possible service by the Cape, with ships that had no first class but could carry 1,100 third-class passengers each.

As for Sutherland, those early chairmen and directors were long-lived. Anderson had led the company for 31 years, from its founding to 1868. Sutherland led it for 46, and man and boy he served it for 60 years until he retired as Managing Director in 1914, and as Chairman a few months later. However, in that year, not long before the beginning of World War I, there were headlines in the newspapers which astounded the City of London and the shipping world.

Sir Thomas Sutherland GCMG (1834–1923), who as Managing Director and later Chairman guided P&O's fortunes for forty-two years, and then engineered the handover of power to Lord Inchcape, Chairman of the British India Company. (Oil by John Singer Sargent, 1898)

9

MERGER AND EXPANSION

Fusion of Two Great Shipping Lines – P and O and British India – Far-Reaching Agreement'. This was the headline of *The Times*' report of 23 May 1914, the day after the news had astonished the City. There was to be 'a complete fusion of the business by means of an interchange of stock. The intention is that the two companies shall be continued as separate entities, but their interests will become identical. It is understood', the newspaper added, 'that negotiations were carried on solely between Sir Thomas Sutherland and Lord Inchcape.'

At a special general meeting of the proprietors, Sutherland explained the amalgamation. British India's (BI) routes were conveniently complementary to those of P&O: managed from Calcutta, the great majority of its ships provided cargo, passenger and mail services across the Indian Ocean, the Persian Gulf and Southeast Asia. They rarely ventured west of Suez, and as *The Times* remarked, 'Those who have not travelled in the East would hardly realize that the British India is the largest individual British shipping line.' So it was, numerically. It owned 131 steamers totalling 598,203 gross registered tons (grt); P&O owned 70, of 548,564 grt. 'What, after all, does this great operation mean?' Sutherland asked the proprietors rhetorically. 'It means that we command the employment of a capital of £15 million ... and this capital and this tonnage will be working with a common aim and purpose for the prosperity of a great national enterprise.' There were murmurs of approval, repeated loudly when he called the amalgamation 'a policy of the most vital character ... in the interest of British commerce throughout our Eastern empire'. But he had another announcement to make, as startling as the amalgamation itself. Without consulting anyone else, he had decided to retire as Chairman, in favour of Lord Inchcape.

Sutherland by then was 78 years old, and had spent all his working life with P&O. Inchcape was 16 years younger, a self-made man of ambition and brilliance. Born James Lyle Mackay, he had been a peer for only three years; his father, a merchant sea captain, drowned when the boy was 12. Thereafter, young Mackay's first jobs had been with a solicitor, with a ropemaker and as a clerk, until in 1874 he was offered a three-year post as General Assistant with Mackinnon Mackenzie & Company. Since 1856, the year they founded BI as the Calcutta and Burmah Steam Navigation Company, Mackinnon's had been its managing agents for British India in Calcutta. Mackay accepted the offer, and stayed in India until 1893.

In his 19 Indian years he became Sheriff of Calcutta, President of the Bengal Chamber of Commerce, and a Commercial Member of the Viceroy's Council. When he was recalled to London, far from being a

The Hughly, Calcutta No. 8.   BOURNE & SHEPHERD

General Assistant, it was as a director of BI. Within another year he gained a knighthood, and in 1901, after the Boxer rebellion, he was sent as plenipotentiary to negotiate a commercial treaty with China. The treaty was signed, but failed through Great Power disagreement; yet the rare failure did Sir James no visible harm. Much semi-official Government work culminated in 1909 with the offer of becoming Viceroy of India. However, the offer was semi-official too, and because of his wide business interests in India it was withdrawn, to his immense disappointment. But compensation came quickly, with a peerage; in 1911, he became the first Baron Inchcape.

Until the announcement of 22 May, no one had had the first inkling that discussions on union were under way. Negotiations – which Sutherland mentioned had begun on 3 March – had been conducted in complete secrecy, man to man. No one has ever been certain who made the first move – on 22 May, Sutherland said he did, but later it was said that the initiative was Inchcape's. Possibly both men had the same idea at the same time, for it was a good idea, and would have been obvious to both. In any event, when the motion was put to the proprietors on 24 June, it was passed with only two dissentients. Neither name was recorded but one of them may have been a Mr Lloyd, who, in the course of the meeting, was vulgar enough to ask how much Lord Inchcape would be paid. Perhaps Mr Lloyd was irritated at the complete lack of consultation. Lord Inchcape's salary was not revealed; but except for the two dissentients, no one objected at all, either to the secrecy or the resulting deal. The first was the expected way of doing things; the second was an eminently suitable outcome.

Calcutta, P&O's Indian terminus in 1842, became BI's headquarters in 1856 and the centre of a network of coastal and deep-sea passenger and cargo shipping. Here, shortly before the First World War, vessels load and discharge both alongside jetties and out in the Hughly.

Looking forward to 1 October, when he would take his seat as a Managing Director on the Board of P&O, Lord Inchcape must have known in the summer of 1914 that war was coming in Europe, that Britain would be involved, and that his ships, and those of P&O, would be called on to serve. Indeed, both companies maintained some vessels as troop carriers on periodic charter to the Government. But he can hardly have guessed that long before the end of 1914, 100 P&O and BI ships would have been requisitioned; 60 ships would have carried troops from India to Europe; two ships would have been lost in enemy action; and one would have been in action against land forces.

On 5 August, within 24 hours of World War I's outbreak, the first requisitioning took place: at Penang, P&O's *Himalaya* – the second of the name – was ordered to Hong Kong for fitting out with eight 4.7-inch guns. Built in 1892, she was an old ship when she was requisitioned but an active role was planned for her: to become an armed merchant cruiser, protecting commerce and patrolling the China Sea.

In Britain, at the same time, the passenger liners *Mantua* and *Macedonia* were transformed into AMCs, and their conversion was completed when the war was only nine days old. On 22 August, the first convoy of troop carriers left India for Suez and Alexandria. Five of the troopers were BI ships; in the second convoy, leaving Bombay and Karachi on 1 September, 13 ships belonged to BI. For the third convoy, on 20 September – the largest to leave India during the war – the company provided 18 vessels, and another 24 were included in the fourth convoy, of 16 October. In that single sailing, BI alone carried 30,000 Indian soldiers and their officers to France: the beginnings of the vast statistics of World War I.

So far the united companies had operated swiftly, efficiently and without physical loss. Certain that speed and efficiency would be maintained as far as conditions allowed, they were equally certain that their happy freedom from loss of ships, lives and cargoes would not continue. For the months of August and September alone, P&O paid £31,000 premium for war-risk insurance of the fleet, and it seemed all too probable that the united companies' first loss would be a P&O ship, somewhere in the Mediterranean or the English Channel. But it was not: instead, on 19 October, far off in the Arabian Sea, between India and Arabia, the BI steamer *Chilkana* fell victim to one of the most successful raiders of that war, the German light cruiser *Emden*.

Emden was a member of the squadron commanded by Admiral von Spee, and her war career lasted only 14 weeks; but in that time, under her captain, Karl von Müller, she captured or sank 23 merchant vessels totalling 101,182 tons. *Chilkana*'s crew could count themselves lucky: von Müller was a seaman of an old tradition, who did everything he could to avoid casualties, and cared well for his prisoners. Ships were his target, not people, and no one in *Chilkana* died.

Commerce raiding – *guerre de course*, as the French called it – was a belligerent practice as old as sea war. Much used by both the French and the Americans in their eighteenth- and nineteenth-century wars against Britain, it was well understood as a method for a weak navy to annoy a strong one. But in the twentieth century, a new phrase – surface raider –

In 1914, when it merged with P&O, the British India Company was the largest British shipping line, owning 131 steamers. The 7,009-ton *Karoa*, completed in 1915, was a typical BI passenger/cargo liner. She served as a troopship during the First World War before joining the Bombay/Seychelles/East Africa service.

had to be invented to describe vessels like *Emden*, for in the previous 20 years or so, sea warfare had been through a revolution. Several major changes had taken place at roughly the same time: mines, originally called torpedoes, had been developed from crude prototypes in the American Civil War into cheap, efficient and deadly weapons. Submarines had likewise developed, though their range, speed and submerged times were still limited. With them, their characteristic weapon, the self-propelled torpedo, had come into being. Apart from going underwater in a way which one British admiral called 'damned un-English', naval warriors had also taken to the air. For decades to come, advocates of air power and supporters of battleships were locked in debate; but in 1914 even the most reactionary had to acknowledge that an aircraft could be a valuable scout and target spotter, extending the eyes of a fleet over the horizon. And finally there were the battleships themselves, changed almost beyond recognition since the Russo-Japanese War of 1904–5. At the battle of Tsushima in 1905, the Japanese inflicted a stunning defeat on the Russian navy, and in direct consequence Admiral Lord Fisher had transformed the Royal Navy. Looking at the nation's capital warships, he growled 'Scrap the lot!' and instituted the creation of two entirely new kinds of vessel: the all-big-gun battleship and the battle-cruiser. The battle-cruiser could outrun anything it could not outshoot; the all-big-gun battleship could outshoot anything on the surface.

These developments of the fighting Navy affected the Merchant Navy profoundly. Around the British coast in those early months of the war, mines were one of the gravest fears for a merchantman: shipping

BI's 7,400-ton *Rohilla* was
taken up as a hospital ship
when war broke out. She was
wrecked off Whitby in a gale
on 1 November 1914 when
bound for Belgium; two lives
were lost.
(Front page of the *Daily
Mirror*, 2 November 1914)

THE DAILY MIRROR, Monday, November 2, 1914.

OUR MONSTER BIRTHDAY NUMBER.
The Daily Mirror

LATEST CERTIFIED CIRCULATION MORE THAN 1,000,000 COPIES PER DAY

No. 3,440. | Registered at the G.P.O. as a Newspaper. | MONDAY, NOVEMBER 2, 1914 | 24 PAGES. | One Halfpenny.

IMPRISONED ON WRECKED HOSPITAL SHIP: MEN JUMP INTO RAGING
1903-1914   SEA AND SWIM FOR THEIR LIVES.   1903-1914

The *Rohilla* being broken to pieces by the waves. Several men are standing on the bridge, while one of them is seen dropping into the water to try and fight his way to the shore. Note the lifeline which fell across the rigging too far away to be reached.—(*Daily Mirror* photograph.)

Rescuers helping a man ashore. Arrows are pointing to others who have nearly reached safety and who were afterwards landed.—(*Daily Mirror* photograph.)

Bound on an errand of mercy to Belgium, the British hospital ship Rohilla was wrecked in a terrible gale on the rocks off Whitby. One lifeboat rescued thirty-five persons, but the others failed to reach the vessel though the gallant crews cheerfully risked their own lives in the attempt. Realising that their only hope was to jump for it several men dived into the sea from the doomed vessel, though not all of them reached the shore alive. The remaining fifty survivors were rescued yesterday.

lanes were well established; unavoidable narrows, such as harbour
entrances, were easily made into deathtraps; and, perhaps worst, mines
were completely indiscriminating. On 1 November 1914, all those
factors appeared to combine in the united companies' second loss. On
that day the BI steamer *Rohilla*, a hospital ship, sank off Whitby, with
the loss of two lives. As she was a hospital ship, the deaths and sinking
seemed worse than an ordinary accident, and for years some still
believed she had struck a mine. In fact, she had run aground, but
national propaganda and the climate of fear made that too simple a
cause. Yet though the 'mine' which sank *Rohilla* was mythical, the
threat posed by mines was all too real.

Three months after *Rohilla*'s loss, Germany announced unrestricted submarine warfare against all vessels approaching the British coast. There was little the companies could do to protect their vessels actively, apart from zigzagging in danger zones (which all ships began doing in the winter of 1914) and sailing in unlit convoy. According to the 1907 Geneva Convention, putting guns on a merchant ship placed it in a different category, making it liable to legitimate attack. Nevertheless, ships still in the company's control did take part in occasional action – such as the improbable adventure of BI's *Bharata* in November 1914.

With three other BI vessels as transports, and the P&O steamer *Karmala* as headquarters, *Bharata* left Bombay in mid-October carrying Indian troops and artillery for an expedition against German East Africa (now Tanzania). The military side was a fiasco; the troops were lucky that the civilian ships and their crews were able, and very willing, to pull them out. The army's planning and intelligence was so deficient that, although the night landing a mile and a half from the town of Tanga was successful, the soldiers woke up to find themselves faced by 'a mass of bush so thick that in places it was not possible even by daylight to see more than five yards ahead'. An attempted advance was repelled and, after an interval, tried again. By then it was quite obvious that the six mountain guns carried in *Bharata* could not possibly be landed; so they were lashed onto her boat deck, and with *HMS Fox*, *Bharata*'s unlikely battery was used to bombard the town. Despite coming under fire from the shore, the ships' bombardment enabled troops to advance close to the town – which by then, not surprisingly, was well warned and prepared. Now the army discovered they had not enough launches and lighters to evacuate the troops; and it was not at all clear what they would have done, had 24 officers from the BI steamers not volunteered themselves and their lifeboats to carry away the dead, the wounded and the survivors. Seven thousand chastened soldiers were rescued in that manner; and, if he had not had the sense to plan properly, at least the general officer commanding had the courtesy to thank BI officially.

Centuries ago a merchant ship could be converted to a warship quite easily. Civilian ships and the king's ships were in most ways similar; armament was elementary and armour unheard of. But since the advent of the steam engine, the explosive shell, the iron and then the steel hull, no merchantman could ever make a thoroughly satisfactory warship again. Nevertheless, in both World Wars British ships were taken up from trade not only to act as transports but as warships too, known as armed merchant cruisers. Inadequately armed and scarcely armoured at all, they patrolled, blockaded, bombarded and fought – acting in every way, indeed, as if they were real warships, and not thin-skinned vessels intended only for peace. Their captains, and probably the majority of their crews, would be Royal Navy men but often their peacetime commanding officer would remain, with the rank of Commander RNR, as navigating officer, accompanied by other volunteers from the peacetime crew. Such men were exceptionally brave: there was always a chance that an unarmed merchant ship would not be attacked. But the very weakness of an armed merchant cruiser, on the

P&O's second *Himalaya* (6,898 tons, built in 1892) was their first liner to be requisitioned for use in the First World War, in August 1914. She was later compulsorily purchased and became an armed merchant cruiser, a seaplane carrier and then a troopship (Watercolour by W.W.Lloyd, 1892)

other hand, meant that it was at least as likely as an authentic warship to be attacked, and less likely to survive.

The 21-year-old armed merchant cruiser *India* was the first such P&O ship to go. On 8 August 1915 she was in the North Sea, taking part in the distant blockade of Germany, charged with stopping and searching vessels which might be carrying war material to the enemy, when she was torpedoed. A hundred and twenty of her men were killed, including two Sub-Lieutenants, a Lieutenant and a Commander RNR from her peacetime P&O crew. Four months later, on 1 December, the BI steamer *Umeta* was southeast of Malta when she became the first of the united companies' civilian ships to be torpedoed. One life was lost, and the episode barely rated a mention in the newspapers. Seven days afterwards, Lord Inchcape felt able to address the P&O shareholders' annual meeting with some pride: 'Week after week,' he said, 'with unfailing regularity, without exception, all through these 16 months of war, the P&O mail steamers have started on their voyages from this country to the far ends of the earth with their usual complement of passengers, just as in times of peace.'

It was certainly a considerable achievement – indeed, P&O's mail service was not restricted at all until June 1917 – and Inchcape underlined the extraordinary luck that went with it. Since *India* had been under Admiralty control and *Umeta* had been a BI ship, he congratulated the P&O meeting on the 'complete immunity' their own ships had so far enjoyed. Ascribing this to the guidance of the Admiralty and the protection of the Navy, he thanked both; but given that he was chairman of BI as well as P&O, his remarks may have conveyed to some shareholders a distasteful appearance of complacency. Certainly he himself felt he might be tempting fate, because he added: 'Of course, we cannot tell when some disaster may overtake us.' Happily so; for, not being prophets, he and the shareholders could enjoy Christmas, and even the New Year as well. The news about *India*'s sister ship *Persia* did not arrive until 3 January.

It seems astonishing today, but in spite of the war, P&O and many other shipping lines continued to publish sailing dates and ports of call. *Persia* was no exception: well in advance it was announced that she would leave London on 18 December for Marseilles, leaving that port Christmas Day for Bombay and Karachi. A 7,974-ton steamer capable of 18 knots, she was carrying 501 passengers and crew, and between 20,000 and 30,000 bags of mail on that voyage. It was her last.

At lunchtime on 30 December she was 40 miles southeast of Crete. The passengers – among them, Lord Montagu of Beaulieu and Robert McNeely, newly appointed American consul to Aden – had just finished their soup when 'the track of a torpedo was observed by Second Officer Wood, four points on the port bow, one second before impact.' There had been no warning. The torpedo struck abaft Number Three Hatch, opposite the boiler room. With the torpedo, the forward port boiler blew up, and the ship began to sink fast.

'The end was a horrible scene', wrote one survivor. 'The water was as black as ink. Some of the people were screaming, others were saying goodbye to each other...' Lord Montagu agreed that it was 'a dreadful scene of struggling human beings. There was hardly any wreckage to grasp. Nearly all the boats were smashed.'

Two boats full of people were drawn down with *Persia*. One diner, rushing on deck, was caught around the leg by a rope and dragged under. Freeing himself, he burst out of the water to see the ship bows up and sinking; within five minutes of the attack she had gone.

Lord Montagu, though he did not think it at the time, was one of the fortunate ones. Swimming to an upturned and damaged boat, he clung to it with three other Europeans and 28 Lascars; and there he hung for 32 hours, without food or water. Three separate vessels passed by, but, fearing the boat was a ruse set by a U-boat, they did not stop. One by one Montagu's unexpected companions died, until there were only 11 left, and he himself was pondering 'how best an Englishman might die when there were Lascars to watch his end'.

He survived, to read his own premature (and very complimentary) obituaries but of the other 500 people on board *Persia*, 335 died. It was the worst single disaster suffered by P&O in the Great War. For days the press was filled with reports and conjecture on the culprit's identity – German, Austrian or perhaps Turkish. In one way that mattered little: the tragedy was a 'prompt illustration of the practical value of assurances and promises given by the Teutonic Allies', and each was as bad as the next; but through the nation, people hoped it might finally bring President Wilson and the United States into the war. For P&O, it marked the end of 'immunity': a dozen more company vessels were sunk before the Armistice – but none, at least, with such great loss of life.

Ships of P&O and subsidiary companies were sunk further north than

Shetland and as far south as the Tasman Sea, in the mid-Atlantic and off Bombay, from Gibraltar to Port Said. Some established astonishing records of escape or survival: *Nellore* had nine separate encounters with submarines and emerged unscathed from them all; *Sardinia* had part of her bows blown off and yet, with water up to the orlop deck, managed to steam backwards for 61 miles to harbour in Oran. Some displayed conspicuous sang-froid: *Mongolia* had exercised emergency drill so often that when she sank in only 13 minutes after being torpedoed near Bombay, lady passengers took to the boats 'chatting and laughing as if starting for a picnic'. And conspicuous valour: *Otaki*, armed with a single 4.7-inch gun, was caught by the surface raider *Möwe*, armed with six large guns, one small one and two torpedo tubes. A long duel ensued, in which the German captain wrote: 'She has luck and an extremely good gunner on board.... The enemy has scored a bull's-eye. Nobody had thought of such a thing.... Our situation is far from happy; the enemy lies there, refusing to sink, and firing shot after shot.' Inevitably *Otaki* did sink but she sank with her single gun still firing and left *Möwe* ablaze and badly damaged. And though her commanding officer, Archibald Smith, had had no naval rank, his bravery deserved the highest recognition. Posthumously, he was gazetted Lieutenant RNR, and was awarded the VC.

The 9,575-ton *Otaki* had only been connected with P&O for nine months when, half-way between the Azores and Newfoundland, she met her end on 10 March 1917. She belonged to the New Zealand Shipping Company, but in June of the previous year, that company and the subsidiary Federal Steam Navigation Company had been bought by P&O – the first of a rapid series of mid-war acquisitions organized by Lord Inchcape. As Vice President of the Institute of Shipbrokers, he was a member of the Government's War Risks Advisory Committee before the outbreak of war, and at the outbreak chaired a committee to agree rates of hire of vessels to the Government. The agreed figures, known as the Blue Book rates, were essentially those of pre-war days; but, while Blue Book rates stayed the same, costs of shipping spiralled, most noticeably coal and insurance. In 1914, P&O's war-risk insurance for 1915 was computed at £180,000. It turned out to be £250,000 – potentially a crippling amount, for many ships were earning less than their insurance costs, quite apart from fuel, salaries, maintenance and repair. Despite the nation's horrific losses to submarines – 2.75 million tons' displacement were sunk in the first six months of 1917 – Inchcape never seemed to doubt that eventually Germany would be defeated. Faith in an Allied victory joined with foresight for the post-war world: a revival of trade would be certain. With preparation, P&O could reap much benefit; without preparation, made vulnerable by wartime losses and expenses, the company could wither. Buying other carefully chosen shipping lines simultaneously diluted the risks of war and paved the way for business afterwards; in the second half of 1917, P&O acquired interests in the Union Steamship Company of New Zealand, the Hain Steamship Company and James Nourse Ltd. Together they added not only 107 vessels of over 370,000 tons to the combined fleet, but also their established trading areas and routes: from Hain's, based in Cornwall,

(Opposite above)
'*Otaki* fighting to the last' in action against the German surface raider *Möwe*, 10 March 1917. New Zealand Shipping Company's 7,420-ton refrigerated cargo liner put up a gallant action against heavy odds, and was officially considered unlucky not to have sunk her assailant.

(Opposite below)
Her back broken, BI's 5,235-ton *Shirala* folds up and sinks after striking a mine off Littlehampton on 2 July 1918. She is wearing the 'splinter' camouflage widely adopted during the war.

(Below)
Like BI, P&O contributed units of its fleet to be hospital ships during the First World War. Here *Plassy* takes on survivors from *HMS Lion* after the Battle of Jutland on 31 May 1916.

During the War the Government requisitioned the Hamburg America Line offices in Cockspur Street in London's West End. P&O bought them at the end of the War, and kept a passenger office there until the early 1970s.

with its 27 ships and worldwide tramp trade, to the Nourse Line, trading between India, the West Indies and Fiji, and on to Union Steam, linking New Zealand, Australia and the Pacific islands across to Vancouver.

Yet though risks were spread and routes were gained, 1917 was an appalling year for the newly extended group. Forty-four ships were lost altogether, to submarines, mines, gunfire, bombs and surface raiders – a total of 284,716 gross tons. A further 14, totalling over 89,000 gross tons, went in 1918 – the last, BI's *Surada*, was torpedoed just nine days before the Armistice. Nevertheless, Inchcape's plan – not only for survival but for revival and expansion as well – was making confident progress. At the start of the war, P&O and BI together owned some 1.1 million tons of ships. Through the war, the combined fleets lost over half a million tons; at the time of the Armistice, they still contained over $1\frac{1}{2}$ million. With the Chairman's general strategy clear, it was hardly surprising that in September 1918, a speculators' rumour that P&O was about to buy Cunard was entirely believed. For a couple of days, some quick profits were made, until Inchcape publicly denied the rumours. The speculation, however, was not so very far wrong; for at the same moment, negotiations were under way for the purchase of the Orient Line, bought at the end of 1918, and the Khedivial Mail Line, acquired in 1919. The Inchcape acquisitions did not stop there: in 1920 the

General Steam Navigation Company was bought, followed in 1923 by the Strick Line. By then, P&O's worldwide shipping interests approached some 500 vessels.

After the ordeal of war, peace in a reshaped world posed its own challenges. Whatever else the war had achieved, one simple truth had been proved and at the time, people thought it could never be forgotten again. In peace or war, the island nation was utterly dependent for its survival on overseas trade. In peace, in some ways it did not matter under which flag the merchantmen sailed but in war the Red Ensign was vital. As Inchcape himself said in the last weeks of war, 'The past 50 months have, at any rate, been a transparent object lesson in the belligerent utility of a service that has transported to five different fronts and kept fully provisioned and equipped many millions of fighting men, besides supplying Great Britain with her essential foodstuffs and war materials.'

The tremendous strategic value of a civilian fleet could not be denied. However, Inchcape feared that short-sighted or laggardly politicians might effectively encourage the destruction of Britain's merchant navy, by not returning ownership swiftly to the owners. Other nations would certainly make hay at British expense – indeed, two had already done so during the war. One of them, America, even provided an example of Inchcape's fear. At the beginning of the American Civil War, the nation's merchant fleet totalled some 2.5 million tons. When that war ended four years later, the figure had dropped by two-thirds to 800,000 tons. Some of the balance had been sunk but the majority had fled or been sold to foreign flags; after the war, stupidly, Congress had not allowed those ships to return. In the meantime Britain took over much of the carrying trade and the American merchant marine did not revive for three generations – that is, until the opportunity presented by the Great War. Similarly, in 1914 Japan's national merchant navy totalled around 1.7 million tons – little more than P&O's combined fleet alone. Allied to Britain since 1902, Japan had made only a limited contribution to the war but had gained at least one considerable benefit: ownership of the ex-German Pacific island groups of the Marshalls, Carolinas and Marianas. Moreover, its merchant fleet had expanded to nearly 3 million tons; and, of course, its natural area of operations overlapped heavily with the areas P&O had been obliged to neglect.

In a strongly argued public letter, Lord Inchcape listed the four major post-war problems facing P&O and the entire British Merchant Navy. Firstly, while America and Japan grew, Britain had lost between 20 and 25 per cent of its merchant fleet. Secondly, since all British shipyards had been fully occupied with building standard cargo vessels for the Government, civilian ships had had no repairs or overhauls during the war. Those, and reconversion from their war role, would take many months. Thirdly, rising foreign competition had weakened the British hold on pre-war markets and routes; and finally, building costs, running costs and taxes had all risen dramatically. Bad as the prospect was, he was sure it could all be coped with, 'if – but only if – the paralysing influence of Government control is removed from the industry at the earliest possible moment.'

Another threat lay in a looming surplus of Government war shipping. Apart from its own standard cargo vessels, produced in great quantity during the conflict, the Government had some 300 ex-enemy ships which it was keen to sell. Inchcape was asked to sell them. There was no way the Government could have been persuaded to scrap the vessels: they were worth scores of millions of pounds. Inchcape personally handled the sales of 496 ships – 3.3 million tons – and 98 of them were bought by the P&O group. Twenty-eight of those were ex-German or ex-Austrian prizes; BI had acquired an ex-German prize as early as 1915. The other 70 were standard-design ships: P&O itself had six of them, BI 40, Hain 15, Union Steam four, Khedivial three and New Zealand Shipping two.

Lord Inchcape's worst fears were not realized – or not immediately. The return of vessels from Government to private ownership was as swift as possible and, for a few years at least, there was ample trade for everyone. Every war creates its trade famine and every peace, however flawed, creates its boom. For P&O, the ten years following the Armistice were prosperous, fuelled by three main factors: the backlog of trade, the renewal of brisk passenger traffic generally, and the great rise in emigration from Britain to America, Canada, Australia and New Zealand, as young families sought new lives beyond the seas. The company's credit balance rose from just over £651,000 in 1919 to break the million mark by 1924, and hovered close to that level during the rest of the 1920s. Dividends, from 1919 to 1924, were regularly 12 per cent, sometimes with added bonuses; and for Lord Inchcape personally, those years, the heady decade of *The Great Gatsby*, brought further distinction – proud, but also comical.

In October 1921, to his complete astonishment, the 68-year-old lord was offered the chance of a lifetime: no less than a monarchy. That he turned it down, despite his lifelong ambition for success and power, is less astonishing – for the crown in question was the crown of Albania. 'Not in my line', he remarked, and courteously refused the honour, which is rather a pity. Probably he would have been quite a good king, though possibly somewhat autocratic and hard; and it is fascinating to speculate on what the history of Albania, and its present relations with the West, might have become if he had accepted. But *The Prisoner of Zenda*, published in 1894, and its sequel *Rupert of Hentzau* probably put him off as much as anything else. British titles counted for something, after all. For others there was a sliding scale, in which Albania figured very low.

The years held more titles in store for him. Three years after the Albanian offer came the offer of a normal, recognizable British viscountcy – much more in his line, and he accepted it. Five years after that, an earldom was proffered and naturally he accepted that too – it would have been nonsense for him to have done otherwise.

The first Earl of Inchcape could remark truthfully that life had brought him many rewards and that he had worked for every one of them; at a time when many people did so, he had not even bought his peerage. He had worked well for P&O too: the company had not only survived the greatest war in history, but, through his own foresight and

(*Opposite*)
After the First World War many people sought new lives in Australia. P&O's Branch Service – the former Blue Anchor Line route – carried hundreds of thousands of emigrants until the early 1930s.

commercial skill, had come out of it stronger than it went in, and was still growing. But there were forces from which even an earl, even the Earl of Inchcape, was not exempt. In 1925, just after he became a viscount, it became evident that peace in the Far East was in severe danger, as the infant republic of China faced civil war between communists, nationalists and rival warlords, as well as external aggression from Japan – all of which touched close on the company's trade. The ermine came to him in 1929 but on 24 October of that year,

The Rt. Hon. the Earl of Inchcape GCSI, GCMG, KCIE (1852–1932), in full ceremonial robes of the Order of St Michael and St George, one of many honours attained over years of service to commerce and his country. How would P&O have fared had he not been barred from the Viceroyalty of India? (Oil by P.A. de Lazlo, 1931)

the Wall Street Crash began. It was the American republic's tenth financial crisis, and the worst – prices had never fallen so fast or so far. And he was getting old. In November 1931, he went to observe the trials of P&O's latest vessel, the 14,500-ton, 20-knot, turbine steamer *Carthage*, whose sister *Corfu* was just undertaking her maiden voyage. The trials were a success and Lord Inchcape accepted the ship into the company's fleet. In doing so, however, he caught a severe chill and came away from the trials feeling weak and tired. He left the country to recover and recuperate in his yacht *Rover*, moored in the Mediterranean. A few weeks later his son-in-law, the Hon. Alexander Shaw, read P&O's proprietors the Earl's address – a despondent note, fitting to the times: 'I have never known such a period of depression as that through which we have passed in the last 18 months', he said. 'It has been heart-rending to see the steamers leaving London, week after week ... with thousands of tons of unoccupied space – so different from the old days.'

It was sad to hear such words from the old man. But sad as they were, they were realistic; for once, everyone could agree that 'the old days' was not just an old man's phrase. China was in turmoil; Germany was becoming more and more disturbing; unemployment at home had reached the burdensome figure of 1.8 million; trade and profits were sliding away. Clearly the old days were gone, and it was somehow appropriate that after his long, active, vivid life – much of it, in his view, in the service of the British Empire – Lord Inchcape died on 24 May 1932, Empire Day.

He was on board his yacht *Rover* at the time, in Monte Carlo. As *The Times* reported: 'Ten minutes before he died, he was enjoying the sunshine on deck.' In an article on the political situation in Europe, the newspaper's adjoining column noted there was no sign of a coalition in the new Prussian Diet between the Catholic Centre and the Nazis. Quoting from a German paper, it added that the only question was whether 'the present crisis of the "system" shall be solved by peaceful means or by force'. Perhaps it was a good time to leave. But to those who remained in P&O, 1932 held one more blow, the clearest sign that times had changed. In the proprietors' meeting of December that year, for the first time since 1867, the directors could not pay a deferred dividend.

10

ENDURANCE

The company's credit balance had plunged by 75 per cent in eight years, from the million-plus of 1924 to £281,000, and every penny had to be ploughed back. There could be no dividend for the foreseeable future; nor could there be any new shipbuilding. Salaries throughout the company had already been cut by 10 per cent in 1931. Taking his seat as Chairman of P&O in 1932, the Hon. Alexander Shaw reflected that the first essential for the company was simply to endure. Any firm may have a down-turn in its fortunes while others prosper, and may need some change in management, product or service, to revive. Yet, in the depressed world of the 1930s, P&O's trading decline was not the exception but virtually the rule. The key, then, was endurance.

The lack of dividend and the salary cuts had to be accepted; few shareholders or employees were going to try and change horses when every other one was up to its neck as well. And, if not optimism, there was at least a sound basis for hope: the fleet itself. Born in 1883, the first son of Lord Craigmyle, Shaw married Lady Margaret Mackay – Inchcape's eldest daughter – in 1913. Seven years later he was elected to the company's Board of Directors and had seen at first hand the decisions which led to his father-in-law's building programmes of the 1920s.

First acquisitions after the war were the six Government Standard ships, and two passenger liners – the 16,000-ton *Naldera* and *Narkunda* whose completion World War I had delayed. But then the real building began; and, capitalizing on the post-war wave of emigration, the first vessels were 13,000-ton one-class ships, each taking around 500 passengers to their new worlds. A company milestone came in 1923, when *Mooltan* and *Maloja* became P&O's first ships registered at over 20,000 tons. Two years later, a major building programme produced the first of the C class, *Cathay*, *Comorin*, *Chitral* and *Corfu*, averaging 15,000 tons each, as well as the 16,000–17,000-ton R class – *Rajputana*, *Ranchi*, *Ranpura* and their famous, ill-fated sister *Rawalpindi*. Hard on their heels came four fast cargo vessels, owned and operated by Hain's, whose running costs were lower than those of P&O, but used on P&O's Far East service. But the company's most successful single vessel of the decade came in 1929: the *Viceroy of India*.

For P&O, *Viceroy* was a bench-mark ship. Just short of 20,000 grt, she was powered by turbo-electric drive. Contrary to the company's usual custom of letting other people experiment, this was a relatively untried novelty, steam turbines powering electric motors, 17,000 horsepower producing 19 knots more smoothly and more quietly than ever before. Apart from that, *Viceroy of India* brought the traditional P&O liner to new levels of magnificent opulence and comfort. Even in

depression, there was a market for luxury and pampering – for the opportunity to turn a necessary journey into a brief but wonderful break from the drabness one had left and the uncertainty one was approaching. The Inchcape family had a close hand in this: designs for *Viceroy*'s public rooms were done by Elsie Mackay, the third of Lord Inchcape's four daughters, and they were fantastic. Not in the sense of something nightmarish but dreamlike: the First-Class Smoking Room was, simply, the Great Hall of a castle – hammerbeams, crossed swords decorating the walls, a large fireplace with baronial arms above it, comfortable armchairs, rugs and tables; and all afloat. To most people, it was the best of both worlds.

Not surprisingly, *Viceroy* was immensely popular, with her eighteenth-century music room, her dining saloon with its blue

(*Right*)
P&O's *Viceroy of India*,
19,645 tons, was a unique ship
built in 1929 for the Bombay
service to which she brought
new standards of speed,
luxury and, thanks to her
turbo-electric machinery,
quietness.
(Watercolour by J. Spurling,
1928)

(*Opposite*)
Viceroy of India's indoor
swimming pool was P&O's
first; previously, pools had
been rigged on deck and
made from canvas and wood.
Few of her successors has
matched *Viceroy's* opulence.

(*Below*) The 'Scots baronial'
design of the First-Class
Smoking Room aboard
Viceroy of India was the work
of Lord Inchcape's third
daughter, the Hon. Elsie
Mackay. She also produced a
variety of 'period' designs for
the other public rooms.

THE · WHITE · SISTERS

marbled pillars, her Adam-style reading room, and her built-in indoor swimming pool – P&O's first – surrounded by Pompeiian reliefs. Yet even she was to be surpassed in popularity by Lord Inchcape's last initiative, the five liners collectively known as the *Straths*. Launched between 1931 and 1938, they began at 22,283 tons rising to 23,732, and the first, *Strathnaver*, introduced a new, very obvious characteristic which every passenger remembered and most passengers loved. Instead of the traditional black hull and stone-coloured upperworks of P&O ships, the *Straths* were all-white, hull and upperworks, with buff funnels and masts. The company had used this colour scheme only twice before – briefly with *Caledonia* in the mid-1890s, and with *Salsette*, on the tropical Aden-Bombay shuttle between 1908 and 1917. Now, exactly as intended, the buff and brilliant white suggested 'a degree of energy, speed and beauty never before attempted'. The less wealthy passengers found themselves no longer second-class but tourist-class, suggesting (until the word came to mean what it had tried to replace) that they had the time and money literally to tour, rather than having to go cheaply and quickly from one place to another. Externally, power and luxury were further suggested by hulls higher than hitherto, and, in the first two ships of the class, by having three funnels – although only the middle one was real. Internally, the lavish decor of their public rooms matched *Viceroy of India*; and beyond all the outward show, there were three genuine improvements as well. All cabins were provided with running water (although hot was still only available in first class); a rudimentary but valuable air-conditioning system was installed; and at over 20 knots, they were fast, bringing the journey time from London to Bombay down from 16 to 15 days.

Such, then, was the fleet Shaw inherited as Chairman: modern – only three of P&O's 41 vessels were pre-war – stylish and fast, whether they were cargo or passenger ships. Added to the good management of Inchcape's last decade, there had been luck too. Since the war, only two P&O ships had been lost – the 25-year-old *Egypt*, rammed and sunk in thick fog in 1922 while crossing the Bay of Biscay, and *Khiva*, accidentally set ablaze in 1931 and subsequently sold. When *Egypt* went down 96 lives were lost – a dozen passengers and 84 of her crew. They could not be restored; nor, it appeared, could part of the cargo – gold and silver bullion valued at the time of her loss at £1,054,000. Its exact position was unknown; the water was 70 fathoms deep; and Lloyd's paid the insurance claim in full. But ten years later, after seven seasons' effort, the Italian company Sorima found the wreck and brought its precious load back to the surface. Thus, if one chose to see it so, despite the gloom of 1932, the year brought one good omen as well.

Any good sign was welcome. As always, P&O and its subsidiary companies were intimately affected by international politics. In the spring of 1933, Adolf Hitler came to power in Germany. In 1935, Mussolini's troops invaded Abyssinia, and nine BI ships were allocated to the Admiralty for use in support for (completely ineffective) League of Nations sanctions against Italy. In 1937 the world crisis mounted as Japan began eight years of undeclared war against China. Each development touched the shipping trade, at worst with disruption of

(*Opposite above*)
The five *Strath* liners of the 1930s were all white with buff funnels and surpassed even *Viceroy of India* in popularity and the quality of their design and service. They introduced white hull colours as a permanent feature of the P&O fleet, so it is not surprising that they were nicknamed the 'White Sisters'.

(*Opposite below*)
In the days of its black hulls, black funnels and 'stone' upperworks, P&O had a somewhat sober image, so no expense was spared even on more trivial items to accentuate the *Straths*' new image. This 1932 menu card cover exemplifies the approach.

supplies, routes and markets, and at best by stoking nervousness and apprehension. Nevertheless, speed and luxury brought profits slowly back to £487,000, and in 1936 a deferred dividend was paid again. Only 4 per cent, but Shaw was proud of it, and rightly so.

Certainly, an important corner had been turned – not only for shareholders but employees as well, for the salary cuts of 1931 were restored. Yet Shaw himself was unwell and in 1937 his father died. In 1938, on doctors' advice, the new Lord Craigmyle retired as Chairman of P&O. Six years in the chair was brief by company standards, and it was a pity that he had to leave. From his record, he would probably have been a good Chairman however long he had stayed; it was much to his credit to have guided P&O through the testing 1930s. For his successor, though, the 1940s would be infinitely more testing and terrible.

Fifty-four years old in 1938, Sir William Crawford Currie was born in India; went to school in Scotland; university in England; and to work back in India. Thereafter his career was uncannily similar to Lord Inchcape's: from assistant he became a partner in Mackinnon Mackenzie and Company, Sheriff of Calcutta, President of the Bengal Chamber of Commerce, Member of the Legislative Council, and Member of the Council of State. In 1925 he was awarded his knighthood just before his return to Britain, and in 1929 he became President of the Chamber of Shipping. He and P&O were made for each other, and he joined the company as a director soon after Inchcape's death. Coming to a company bereft of its leader and beleaguered by depression, he did not imagine that only seven years later he would be responsible for P&O in a war far worse than the Great War.

In the 20 years since the Treaty of Versailles, merchant ships had grown larger and swifter, more capable of doing their job well. But they were not really any more capable of doing a war job with complete efficiency, and weapons were more deadly than ever. Submarines and their torpedoes could travel farther faster. Though it was not yet known elsewhere, Germany had developed a magnetic mine, far superior to the contact mines of World War I. Under the terms of the Versailles Treaty, the German navy had devised its infamous pocket-battleships, vessels with the tonnage of a cruiser and the fighting power of a battleship – ideal weapons for commerce raiding. Aircraft had been transformed: no longer the ponderous Zeppelins or fragile biplanes of the Great War, they were now huge long-range bombers and speedy, well-armed fighters.

As tension grew between the nations and Chamberlain renounced the policy of appeasement, the possibility of aerial bombardment had to be considered in London. At Croxley Green in Hertfordshire, Currie established an emergency headquarters for P&O, housing duplicates of company records and run initially by a skeleton staff. Physically moving further away from Germany was a natural psychological reaction, and Croxley Green was, of course, a much less likely target than central London. But that, and not distance, was its only practical protection in comparison, for as the crow flies, it is only about 20 miles northwest of Leadenhall Street. However, no one then imagined that one day Coventry and even distant Liverpool might fall victim to air raids.

The starting date of almost any war depends on view-point. An American might say that World War II only began with Pearl Harbor in December 1941, and that before then, it was a European war. A Briton would probably say it began on 3 September 1939 with Chamberlain's declaration, and a Pole would certainly say it began on 1 September, when Hitler's soldiers invaded Poland. But P&O could quite reasonably say that, for the company, World War II began on 24 August 1939, for on that day, *Rawalpindi* was requisitioned.

In the weeks leading up to Japan's attack on Pearl Harbor, British intelligence agents in the Far East predicted correctly the date of that

Sir William Crawford Currie, GBE, (1884–1961) joined the P&O Board early in 1932 and was almost at once appointed Deputy Chairman. He succeeded Lord Craigmyle as Chairman and oversaw the traumas of the Second World War, post-war rebuilding and the beginnings of diversification before retiring in 1960. (Oil by Robert Swann after Edward Haliday)

strike, although neither they nor the Americans predicted the place. The British method was simple: noting that all Japanese merchant ships were being called back to the homeland, they made a graph with ships on one axis and dates on the other. This showed that all merchantmen would be back by 6 December, implying that an attack somewhere would be likely on 7 December or soon after.

In the summer of 1939, no such universal recall of British merchant vessels was politically possible; Hitler could use any 'provocative' act, or any act which could be interpreted as provocative, as his last excuse. So on 3 September the 368 ships of P&O and its subsidiary companies were scattered, as usual, round the globe. However, the British Empire was too – and in Belfast, Bombay, Calcutta, the Cape of Good Hope, Glasgow, London and Esquimault, British Columbia, P&O vessels came for conversion to war. By the end of the month a dozen ships had exchanged the quartered house flag of P&O for the White Ensign.

A typical conversion involved mounting eight 6-inch guns in a ship. It made them sound powerful, at least; but if it had not been pathetic, it would have been ludicrous – the guns were at least 40 years old, relics made before the Boer War of 1899. With these, P&O was sent to war.

Of those first dozen ships, one went to the eastern Mediterranean; one, based on Freetown, assisted on patrolling the South Atlantic; another was allocated to patrol and escort between Bombay and Durban; two went to the Eastern Fleet; and seven joined the Northern Patrol, covering the seas between Greenland, Iceland and Scotland. In the best of weather the last is an unfriendly stretch of water; in autumn or winter, even in peacetime, it can easily be deadly. The ships' duties were to report and intercept all non-Allied ships, to board neutrals, and – if any appeared – to attack enemies. The 14-year-old *Chitral*, *en route* from Scapa Flow to her patrol area, took the opportunity of using an iceberg for target practice, hitting it with every shot. The accuracy was not surprising – the berg was as large as St Paul's Cathedral – but it was a fortifying exercise, all the same.

Out in those wild seas, between the beginning of September and the end of December 1939, ships of the Northern Patrol sent about 250 neutral vessels into port for examination, intercepted 17 German ships and captured one – the other 16 were scuttled by their crews before capture. And in a gallant and terrible encounter, one ship of the Northern Patrol, *Rawalpindi*, was lost.

On 23 November, three months after being requisitioned, *Rawalpindi* was on patrol between Iceland and the Faeroe Islands. By mid-afternoon, dusk was already coming on, with mist over the sea making visibility still poorer, when a very large, vague shape was seen approaching. For some minutes it was difficult to identify; then the men in *Rawalpindi* realized they were about to face the battlecruiser *Scharnhorst*. Laid down with her sister *Gneisenau* in 1935, *Scharnhorst*'s declared 26,000 tons displacement masked a true 32,000 tons. Ten years younger than *Rawalpindi*, her armament included nine 11-inch and twelve 5.9-inch guns; she could do 32 knots; her radius of action was 10,000 miles; and she was making the German Navy's first attempt to break out into the Atlantic. To try and stop her with *Rawalpindi* would

P&O's *Rawalpindi*, serving as an armed merchant cruiser with a Royal Naval Reserve and Volunteer Reserve crew, in gallant but hopeless action against the German battlecruisers *Scharnhorst* and *Gneisenau* in the North Atlantic, 23 November 1939. (Oil by Norman Wilkinson, 1940)

be rather like bicycling towards a tank. Captain E. C. Kennedy, RN, commanding *Rawalpindi*, signalled the sighting to the Home Fleet in Scapa Flow, turned his vessel, and made for the shelter of a fog bank. First by light and then by a shot across the bows, *Scharnhorst*, thinking *Rawalpindi* was an unarmed merchant ship, signalled her to heave to; and at that moment Kennedy sighted *Gneisenau*. The fog bank was unattainable. A third challenge came from *Scharnhorst*, and rather than surrender, Kennedy pedalled his metaphorical bicycle against both enemy vessels, opening fire with his antique guns.

No one on board or on shore would have wanted the alternative but it was a suicidal, crazily brave action. Very quickly, *Rawalpindi* scored at least one hit on *Scharnhorst*. However, both the great warships hit the old liner time after time, and 14 minutes after the first shot she was a dead ship. Captain Kennedy was dead too, and out of the 65 P&O men in her company – a fifth of the total complement – 54 had been killed. Twenty-two were officers, with RNR ranks from Acting Sub-Lieutenant to Engineer Commander. The others filled every humble, necessary role – butcher, baker, steward, chef, scullion, purser, electrician, winchman, pantryman, storekeeper, sick-bay attendant: the jobs they had had in the ship in peacetime. Somehow the very ordinariness of their occupations made their action braver and their deaths more tragic. 'They must have known as they sighted the enemy that there was no chance for them,' said Prime Minister Chamberlain to the House of Commons a few days later, 'but they had no thought of

The 23,000-ton *Straths* were too large to be armed cruisers, so they spent the War years as transports. *Strathaird*, built in 1932 and seen here in pleasanter times, evacuated 6,000 troops and civilians, let alone British gold, from Brest in 1940. (Oil by Derek Smoothey, 1986)

surrender. They fought their guns till they could be fought no more ... their example will be an inspiration to those who come after them.'

The sacrifice had a value in strategic terms as well: alerted by Kennedy's signal, ships of the Home Fleet steamed out, and both the battlecruisers retreated to Germany.

As in World War I, when *Persia* was torpedoed, the deaths in *Rawalpindi* constituted P&O's first and worst single disaster in World War II. Another curious parallel with World War I was that after *Rawalpindi*'s destruction, P&O seemed to have almost complete immunity in World War II's early months, while BI, its sister company, suffered. During 1940, though several of its vessels were exposed in areas of great peril, P&O's only loss was a small coaster which vanished in the North Sea. *Rawalpindi*'s motor launches, removed on her conversion, took part in the evacuation of Dunkirk, as did pleasure steamers from General Steam and its subsidiary, the New Medway Steam Packet Company. *Strathaird* evacuated civilians, children, gold and 6,000 troops from Brest; *Redcar* brought refugees from Norway, *Narkunda* from Marseilles and *Ettrick* from St Jean de Luz. There was another odd parallel in that operation, too. The second Lord Inchcape had died in 1939 and had the first Lord Inchcape made a different decision in 1921, one of the evacuees could have been his grandson. For among the crowd waiting to board *Ettrick*, complete with queen and crown jewels, there was Zog, occupant of the Albanian throne which Inchcape had refused.

In that same month, June 1940, came an echo of even earlier wars, when the first *Himalaya* was destroyed. Built in 1853 and bought by the Government for use in the Crimea, she had long since been sold to a private company which used her as a coal hulk, moored in Portland; and there, she was bombed to bits. By herself, she was not a great loss for anyone, nor a great victory for the Luftwaffe. But in March 1940, BI's *Domala* was bombed and burnt out off the Isle of Wight. In an operation against Narvik in May 1940, BI's *Mashobra* was bombed. After landing troops during the Norwegian campaign, Orient Line's *Orama* was sunk by the German heavy cruiser *Admiral Hipper*; and on 16 September, BI had its third bombing loss of the year, when *Aska* was hit in the channel between Northern Ireland and the Mull of Kintyre.

The names Narvik and British India were clearly fated that year. During the night of 18 November – almost exactly six months after *Mashobra*'s loss in the far north – *Nowshera* was steaming from Calcutta to Australia, when, about 1,000 miles west of Perth, she was stopped by a gun-shot. The German raider overpowered ship and crew with the loss of one British life, took *Nowshera*'s men prisoner, and finally blew the merchantman up with timebombs. And the raider was called *Narvik*.

'Where shall we our breakfast take?' The wreckage of the dining saloon of BI's passenger/cargo liner *Domala* (8,441 tons, built 1921) after she had been bombed off the Isle of Wight on 2 March 1940.

At the beginning of the war, BI ran 22 regular Middle and Far Eastern services, linking Calcutta, Bombay, Singapore, Bangkok, Madras, Karachi, Rangoon, Japan, Australia and the Persian Gulf; and it was in the Persian Gulf that the company had its first direct contact with the war, only a week after its beginning. The little passenger vessel *Barpeta* was chugging harmlessly up the gulf towards Muscat when her master learned from the Navy that an RAF aircraft had crashed somewhere in the Iranian desert. A slow, cautious search, considerably closer to the shore than territoriality allowed, resulted in the rescue of all four airmen, to their own delight – Persia, they reckoned, was 'all sand with no fresh water' – and to the fury of the regional governor, who found out much too late what had been going on.

By Easter 1940, the entire BI fleet of 103 ships – 55 passenger and 48 cargo – was under official direction, either with the Admiralty, the Ministry of Transport, or, in two instances, with the RAF. They were used to the utmost: by the end of 1941, the first 27 months of the war, a single fairly typical ship had made no less than 80 calls at 26 different ports, as far apart as Cape Town, Wellington, Singapore and Gibraltar. Sometimes alone, whenever possible in convoy, they carried food and war supplies, troops, animals and weapons; they became places of haven, crowded with wounded soldiers, or fleeing refugees and evacuees. They were escape routes and lifelines. BI's *Dunera*, a troop carrier throughout the war, transported soldiers from over 100 different units between 1939 and 1945. For its part, P&O contributed 16 troop carriers, which, by the war's end, had convoyed almost a million soldiers to and from battle. During World War I, BI took nearly 84,000 horses from Australia to India, with a mortality rate of less than 4 per cent; and though World War II is thought of as a highly mechanized conflict, the ground forces of both sides still depended heavily on mules and horses. The German Wehrmacht kept meticulous statistics: each of its 90 infantry divisions in 1939 had at least 4,800 horses; some – the poorest, with fewest motor vehicles – had over 6,000; and by the end of the war 2.7 million horses had served them. In the World War I, by contrast, the German army used only 1.4 million horses – little more than half the number of the second, supposedly more sophisticated, World War.

Supporting the need for livestock, BI's workshops at Garden Reach, Calcutta, and the joint P&O/BI Mazagon Dock at Bombay converted nine company ships into animal transports. In the same workshops, *Barpeta* and three other BI vessels were turned into naval auxiliaries. Seven more of the company's fleet were converted there into hospital ships, along with 14 which emerged as troopships and one which became a mine-carrier. Small new specialized vessels were built there as well – river steamers, motorboats, landing craft, minesweepers, patrol boats – and, in the course of the war, thousands of repairs and refits large and small were carried out on damaged craft. Perhaps the most spectacular of those was the repair of a hole 80 feet by 100 feet in the side of a torpedoed steamer; yet though less obvious, the degaussing gear fitted in a further 127 ships was still more valuable. At first by using a giant cradle, later by mounting a cable on the ship, degaussing involved

(*Above*)
On 10 January 1940 the Sydney portion of the first convoy from Australia and New Zealand – *Strathnaver* and four Orient Line ships – sailed for the Near East loaded with troops (*left*). During the war sixteen P&O troopships carried nearly a million troops.
(*Sydney Morning Herald*)

passing an electric current through a cable encircling a vessel's hull. The process counteracted or reversed the vessel's magnetic field, and made it more or less invulnerable to magnetic mines – a marvellous benefit, not only in terms of physical safety, but also in reducing the fear and mental stress of seafaring in wartime. In Tilbury Docks in London, P&O's launch *Faun* participated in the same life-saving service for more than 15,000 vessels, from barges to assault craft, throughout the war.

With 1940 remembered as the year of evacuation, 1941 became the combined companies' first year of severe, sustained loss – five ships from P&O, 13 from BI, and still more from their subsidiary companies. The year had scarcely begun when, on 2 January, BI's *Nalgora* was torpedoed twice off southwest Portugal. On 16 February came a stark lesson in the peril of sailing alone: *Gairsoppa*, heavily laden with pig-iron, could not keep up with her 8-knot convoy, fell out, and was sunk in mid-Atlantic with only one survivor. Three weeks later, a double sinking: P&O's *Lahore* off Freetown, fortunately with no loss of life, and BI's *Nardana* north of the Cape Verde islands. Nineteen died in *Nardana*, 16 of them Indian seamen. Partly because there were more of them and partly because they found it more difficult to withstand cold and exposure, the Indian crewmembers' lists of dead usually far outnumbered the Europeans. In *Gairsoppa*, for example, ten Europeans and 67 Indians died; there were many more before the tragic lists could be closed at last.

P&O's steamer *Somali* was the next victim of 1941, bombed off the Northumberland coast. After her, attention switched to two of the armed merchant cruiser fleet: *Rajputana*, a sister of *Rawalpindi*, torpedoed west of Iceland on 13 April; and one week earlier in the north Atlantic, *Comorin*.

Her loss was unusual; no enemy action was involved but the simple, awful accident of fire in the engine-room. How it started, no one ever knew – it took hold too fast – and soon no one cared, for despite every effort, the flames swept out of control. To be on fire, hundreds of miles from land, with night coming on, a heavy sea running and a gale blowing – for any seaman it is the stuff of nightmare. Added to all this was the plain fact of war: a distress signal could bring an enemy as easily as a friend. Yet a signal had to be sent, and was; and with immense luck and skill, what could have been utter calamity developed into a brilliant, dramatic rescue.

Three ships responded to the signal: the cargo ship *Glenartney* and the destroyers *Lincoln* and *Broke*. Converging on the burning cruiser, they came alongside one by one, and between them took off 425 men. The First Lieutenant of *Broke* painted a picture of the operation. As vividly as is possible in an unmoving image, Sir Peter Scott's painting shows the danger of that night encounter: *Comorin*'s rounded stern rears above *Broke*'s funnels, the cruiser's bulk dwarfing the destroyer, while flame-stained smoke billows downwind into a pitch-black background and wavecrests reflect the blaze. But there are some things impossible to convey in a painting – the icy Atlantic wind, the stink and the blinding sting of the smoke, the fear of death by fire or water, and above all, the motion. Two tiny figures, silhouetted against the glare, leap from the hulk vertically down to the destroyer's deck. But at one moment that deck could be 40 feet below them, and the next, ten feet above, as both ships rolled beam on to the sea; and with each approach by *Broke*, the two hulls would smash together.

Broke's part in the operation lasted four hours, ending after midnight. Before her, *Glenartney* and *Lincoln* had taken as many men as they could. When it was all over, although a quarter of the survivors had been injured, only 20 had been lost. A minor episode, perhaps, in the context of global war – but none the less a triumph.

The sister companies' eighteenth loss of the year was one of the naval auxiliaries converted in BI's Indian workshops, the little *Chantala*. Taking part in the relief of Tobruk, she entered its harbour, struck a mine and sank swiftly. The date has never been forgotten; yet not because of *Chantala*'s small tragedy. It was 7 December – 'a date', said President Roosevelt, 'which will live in infamy' – and as the BI naval auxiliary slid under the waters of Tobruk harbour, Japan entered the war like a thunderclap, and the waters of Pearl Harbor closed over four American battleships.

The *Ranchi*, sister of P&O's doomed *Rawalpindi*, had operated in the East Indies since her conversion to an armed merchant cruiser at the war's beginning. When asked what AMC work out there was like, one of her officers said, 'Hellish hot – and damn dull.' No longer: for as the war suddenly exploded into a truly global conflict, warships and company

6 April, 1941:
'The decks flashed past, and the *Comorin*'s men had to leap as though from an express lift.'
(Oil by Peter Scott, 1941)

ships alike had fewer and fewer zones of safety. BI's *Talamba* rescued many men from the *Prince of Wales* and *Repulse*, delivering them safely to Ceylon. But during 1942, P&O lost ten ships, BI 13, with eight of the BI vessels going down in the newly vulnerable Middle and Far East – the Arabian Sea, the Bay of Bengal and the Strait of Malacca all received their share. During the evacuation of Singapore, two little P&O ships – the 1,000-ton *Mata Hari* and *Bulan*, literally 'the sun' and 'the moon' – carried refugees out of the besieged city-port. *Bulan*, 'the moon', reached Ceylon intact; but, after scurrying from shelter to shelter, to a point east of Sumatra and 400 miles south of Singapore, *Mata Hari* was captured in the Bangka Strait. 'The sun' fell victim to Japan's Rising Sun; and for most of her crew it was the second time around, for she was manned by survivors of the *Prince of Wales* and *Repulse*.

For the allied companies as for the Allied countries, 1942 was the worst year of the worst war they had ever known. Japan's wave of conquest swept out from the homeland even more rapidly than the German *Blitzkrieg* in Europe had done: within weeks, Imperial Japanese forces held undisputed control from the Dutch East Indies to the westernmost Aleutians, from the Gilberts to deep within Manchuria. But, both for the companies and countries, it could have been much worse. The Imperial Navy made one thrust into the Indian Ocean, and then, in accordance with its long-standing plan, turned back to conquer the rich oil-fields and rubber estates of southeast Asia. Yet at that time – with America in disarray, making ready too late; with British Far Eastern forces in retreat; with Madagascar under the control of Vichy France, and North Africa close to being controlled by Germany – Japan could have swept across the Indian Ocean, joined with Germany in the Red Sea, and shattered the majority of Allied lines of supply and communication, from Australia to India, Russia to Africa, Britain to the Middle East. That, however, was the final weakness of the Axis powers: they fought not one World War but two very large separate wars, while for all their arguments of policy and priority, the Allied powers fought one war for a common purpose.

P&O was an essential cog in that effort. In 1942 Sir William Currie became Director of the Liner Division of the Ministry of War Transport, and from there was able to contribute to the planning of the Allies' greatest naval strategies in Europe and North Africa: the invasions of North Africa, Sicily and Normandy.

Operation Torch, the invasion of North Africa, began on 8 November 1942. Training for the operation had taken place on and around Loch Fyne in Scotland, with eight P&O vessels included in the naval force: all five *Straths*, *Mooltan*, *Ettrick* – a purpose-built 11,000-ton troop carrier, able to take 1,150 troops and their officers – and *Viceroy of India*. On 26 October the first convoy of 20 ships sailed, *Strathnaver* leading one column. *Viceroy* was there too, with *Ettrick* and *Mooltan*; P&O's *Cathay* had joined, and so had *Awatea*, from the subsidiary Union Steam Ship Company. In other words, 30 per cent of the convoy came from P&O; and ahead of them, some 40 submarines waited in a pack beneath the Bay of Biscay.

The convoy should not have got through, and on that basis, Torch

should not have been accomplished. But coming up from Africa to Britain was a slow cargo convoy, with P&O's *Nagpore* in it, and those were the ships the submarines found. On 28 October *Nagpore* was torpedoed – an unintended sacrifice and diversion, allowing, by her death, the safe passage of her company-sisters. They steamed through the Strait of Gibraltar on 6 November, and by the night of the 7th they were in position off Algiers and Oran. Within hours troops were landing. Landing continued throughout the 8th; on the 9th the general assault began; and by dusk on the 10th, *Strathnaver*, *Cathay* and *Viceroy of India* were berthed alongside in Algiers harbour. *Strathnaver* would survive – but within 24 hours both *Cathay* and the magnificent *Viceroy* were destroyed.

Viceroy was first, torpedoed in the early hours of 11 November as she steamed homeward. *Cathay* was bombed that same afternoon when assaulting the port of Bougie, 120 miles east of Algiers. The 13,000-ton *Awatea* from New Zealand was destroyed at Bougie too; and before the end of the year, the North African campaign claimed three more P & O ships – *Narkunda*, *Ettrick* and *Strathallan*, all serving as troopships – as well as one BI vessel, *Karanja*, serving as an Infantry Landing Ship. Fifty-four days separated the sinkings of *Nagpore* and *Strathallan*, first and last of the company ships to be lost as a result of Torch: the operation cost P&O and its subsidiaries over 110,000 tons of shipping, 2,000 tons a day. But looking back, it was worth every ton.

It was a great sight – bombs exploding, flares dropping slowly down, then the AA defence guns busy with their snake-like tracers going up.... As dawn came up I verified our position and there was Mount Etna showing up above the smoke. Somewhere about 3.30 a.m. we saw rockets going up which indicated that our men had made a successful landing and obtained their first objective. They gave me quite a thrill, as the coastline had not looked too healthy with so many searchlights and AA guns in action.

So wrote Captain F. Caffyn, the naval officer commanding BI's *Dunera*, when he recalled the events of 9 July 1943: the invasion of Sicily, leading to the invasion of Italy. *Strathnaver* took part as well, as a troop carrier, with three other P&O ships, while BI also contributed a 'mule ship', *Nirvana*, bearing draught animals from South Africa, and four hospital ships. Crews of the latter had no direct means of defence – none of the psychological relief of being able to fire back, however ineffectively – and as one of them remarked, their first experience of an air raid 'brought home to us the peculiar feeling of helplessness in a hospital ship ... and made us all think of what might happen with patients on board'.

But even in the troop carriers and AMCs, guns were of little more than psychological use. They could fend off an attack; yet if a bomb or torpedo struck one of those thin-skinned vessels, it was rare for the ship to survive. 'She became dead, and felt as though she was collapsing like a pack of cards', said one World War I P&O Captain whose ship was torpedoed. Others in World War II echoed and elaborated his words:

There was an almighty ear-splitting crash, the ship shuddered, the light flickered ... there was a roar the like of which I had never heard before – it was catastrophic; it was so awful it was like an unearthly quietness ... the darkness was a hot black cloud, it enveloped one, almost solid in its intensity ... the roar of water rushing into the torn ship was like a thousand express trains tearing through a vast tunnel ...

As in the First World War, BI supplied hospital ships in the Second. *Talamba* (8,017 tons, built 1924) here arrives at Alexandria with wounded British prisoners-of-war being repatriated from Italy, 24 April 1943. She was bombed and sunk on 10 July during the Sicilian campaign.

'It needed some guts', another officer in another sinking ship wrote, 'on the part of the engine crew on that murky night of uncertainty to go down into the bowels of the ship with a big hole open to the sea and carry on firing the boilers, knowing that, if we were hit a second time, there would be little hope of escape.'

Commanding officers were no less frightened, and no less determined: 'It was a queer feeling I had all this time,' said one. 'I felt that everyone on board was watching me, and I hoped that we would be able to pull through.' Remaining on the bridge, he remembered 'feeling rather lonely standing up there alone; but all was going as we had practised hundreds of times before, there was no panic and everyone was being quietly efficient.'

Once in the sea, darkness, cold and shock were the prime enemies; and as one BI survivor remarked, 'What looks like a calm sea from a ship seems like a storm when you are swimming in it.' Yet he was one of the lucky ones: the joint lists of war dead who served with P&O and BI include 250 European names, and the names of no less than 979 Indian seamen.

Following the invasion from the south through Italy came D-Day from the north through France. P&O was there, carrying soldiers, guns, food, fuel and ammunition to Normandy in June and July 1944. *Redcar* in particular served at Juno, Sword and Gold beaches – the entire British landing area. By then, the worst was over for the great shipping company and its associates. P&O itself had no further war losses. BI had only two more – *Neuralia*, mined off Italy on the eve of the German and Italian surrender; and, almost two years later, the final victim of the war's vast minefields, the steamship *Sir Harvey Adamson* disappeared without trace off the coast of Burma, and 55 lives were lost. But that was a future shock, and the companies ended 1945 with relief and rejoicing. *Redcar* was in London on 8 May, and, as was noted in her log, 'No work done this day. VE Day. Port and company's regulations strictly complied with.' At the other geographical extreme, British India's *Vasna* was the first British hospital ship to enter Kure, the port for Tokyo, and the first to go alongside in a Japanese port after the cessation of hostilities. And between the two extremes, but speaking for the ships and men in every port, BI's *Manela* arrived at Madras and 'made a grand entry into the harbour; all the ships were dressed . . . and they all blew their whistles in greeting.'

Nation and company had been intent firstly on survival, secondly on victory; and when both had been achieved and peace regained, another BI man managed to sum up the depression, the war and their stoic endurance: it had been, he said, 'Just one thing after another, but one has a strong will to live.'

11

END OF EMPIRE

On Wednesday 18 December 1946, the proprietors gathered at 122, Leadenhall Street, for P&O's first peacetime annual general meeting in six years. The company's offices had escaped the blitz: 'There have been near misses,' said Sir William Currie, 'but we are delighted to be able to welcome you in this first year of peace to this same old room undamaged, and the same pictures in their usual place.'

It was a comforting image of stability and continuity and Sir William's speech fitted the mood of relieved survival. He gave bad news – the destruction of the company's Singapore offices – matched by good news, amusingly phrased: 'The company's office property in Hong Kong is intact – in fact, it is reported to us that the Japanese effected considerable improvements.' He listed a dismal catalogue of war loss, concluding it with a wry remark: 'In the circumstances, it is to be hoped the travelling public will bear with us if the facilities and opportunites offered are not quite up to pre-war standard in early post-war years.' He indicated a likely new competitor, air travel, and stated his firm belief that 'air and sea can and should be complementary'; and in one sentence he placed the company's plans squarely before the proprietors: 'We intend to build and run within economic limits the best possible service between Great Britain, Australia, India and China.'

It was good forward-looking stuff and very much what the proprietors wanted to hear; their company had survived, and would revive. But no one pretended it would be easy. Company and group losses had been frighteningly large. On 3 September 1939, P&O had owned 21 passenger ships and 15 cargo ships, coastal or deep sea – 36 vessels totalling 460,000 tons. Eleven of the cargo ships had been sunk and eight of the passenger ships – 19 vessels totalling over 190,000 tons. Within the group, Hain's lost its entire fleet of 24 cargo ships. In 1939 the Nourse Line had had six ships and though some survived, several wartime deliveries did not; by 1945, it had lost seven vessels altogether. BI lost 45, half its pre-war total; the Union Line lost a quarter of its 1939 level, and the Strick Line 85 per cent. Overall, the pre-war group had included 371 ships of 2.2 million tons, and by VJ Day, 182 of those – 1.2 million tons, nearly 55 per cent of the original – had gone.

However, things could have been considerably worse. The last great U-boat campaign had ended in 1943, and as America's marvellous 'Liberty' shipbuilding programme got under way – the mass production, in four years, of 2,770 prefabricated vessels amounting to over 29 million tons – much of the strain had been lifted from British yards. At the first opportunity, Currie placed orders for new ships. Only two cargo vessels were built for P&O during the war but by 1945 orders were in hand for another four cargo ships and two fast passenger liners; and

(*Above*)
The P&O Memorial Window in the Seamen's Chapel at All Hallows-by-the-Tower in London. The church was rebuilt after being bombed in the Second World War and re-dedicated in 1957. By now P&O was beginning to think of itself as a group of companies.

(*Opposite*)
P&O's third *Himalaya*, (27,955 tons) was completed in 1949 when there was a very steep post-war rise in shipbuilding costs. Without mail contracts there was no need to replace all P&O's passenger ship losses, but it still needed to rebuild its fleet, especially for the Australian run.

wartime building in the group's other companies was vigorous as well, bringing over 425,000 tons of replacements. Yet the net losses could not be disguised – six years of war had reduced the group's fleet by 111 ships totalling 760,000 tons.

Added to the harsh figures of loss were the abnormally high mileages demanded of, and abnormally low maintenance given to, the ships which had survived. Reconditioning was going to be a lengthy process, and not all the ships were even available for reconditioning at once –

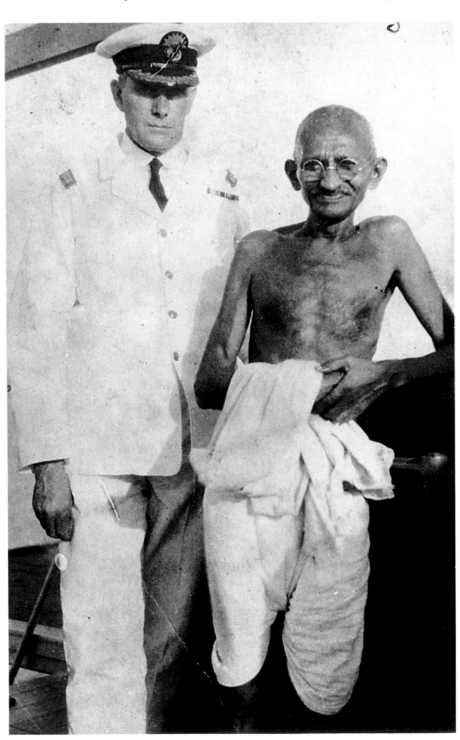

In 1881 an Indian law student, Mahatma Gandhi, had sailed from Bombay to Marseilles in P&O's *Clyde*. Fifty years later he repeated the journey aboard *Rajputana* (he is seen here with Captain H.M. Jack) on his way to the Round Table Conference. Within twenty years the Raj, which the P&O ship represented, was no more; nor were *Rajputana*, torpedoed in 1941, nor Gandhi himself.

after all, soldiers had to be brought home somehow. Not until April 1946 did P&O receive its first cargo ship back from Government requisition. The last P&O liner released after post-war refit was *Strathnaver*, returned on 5 January 1950. Queues at building yards, irregular supplies of rationed materials, and mounting prices of everything only emphasized that if normality was ever going to return, it was still a long way off, down a difficult road.

The end of World War I had brought a sudden steep rise in ship-building prices, as owners scrambled to make good the losses of that conflict. The end of World War II was as bad: by 1947, P&O's first new passenger liner (the third *Himalaya*) was expected to cost £3 million. At 29,000 tons, this represented over £110 a ton – 'an appalling figure, I think you will agree,' said Sir William. The proprietors did agree; they too could remember that a mere ten years earlier, *Canton*, *Strathallan* and *Stratheden* had averaged only £48 a ton. 'The capital cost of new ships has reached such a point', the chairman continued gloomily, 'that it will be a matter of real anxiety as to how we can earn enough to cover overheads, depreciation, plus a small return. . . . It is not enough for a ship merely to earn depreciation equivalent to its original cost; it must earn sufficient to enable a new ship to be built at the higher cost.' There was a strong temptation, in those early post-war years, to hold off from building until prices fell. It had happened in 1923 and a generation later it seemed reasonable to suppose the pattern would repeat itself. Many tramp-shipowners did defer new building but liner owners, with a particular trade to recapture and goodwill to maintain, did not have the choice. They had to build and risk being crippled. The only other alternatives were to shut up shop at once, or slowly fade away. And it was just as well they did build, then and there, however astronomical the costs seemed – for the pattern of 1923 did not repeat itself.

Indeed, the pattern of the company's entire history was changing. Any businessman was accustomed to thinking of shipping as a cyclical industry; most Britons were accustomed to thinking of international politics as a cycle of war, victory, boom, slump, and stabilization, ending with the British Empire strong and pre-eminent as ever. And with P&O's old, intimate connection with the Empire, that was the normality to which the proprietors hoped to return. But in 1947, the year of the company's 110th anniversary, India, the cornerstone of Empire, was granted independence. Inevitably, the numbers of P&O's traditional, steady passengers – soldiers, civil servants and families travelling between Britain and India – would diminish rapidly. Farther east, colony after colony of Britain, France and Holland became independent; one after another, the new nations realized they too could own ships and influence trade, and so – largely for reasons of prestige – they did, with tariffs, import barriers, quotas, and regulations protecting their own shipping. In an altered world, P&O responded by altering the whole balance of its activities.

The one thing unaltered by World War II was the sea. It was still simultaneously a barrier and a means of communication. Aircraft were

(*Overleaf*)
'Line' voyages continued to dominate P&O's passenger operations until jet airliners became an economic reality. Regular line sailings to the Far East ended in 1969, to India in 1970, and to Australia not long afterwards.

The P&O group had to rebuild its cargo liner fleet after the war to maintain its position against growing competition. Ships were larger and faster, too. The 8,199-ton *Salmara* was built in 1956 for P&O's Far East service.
(Acrylic by George Dickinson)

now able to cross the barriers of oceans much faster than any ship but in comparison to their limited, expensive capacity, it was still far cheaper to send any normal freight by ship. From this came one of the most noticeable of the post-war changes in P&O's shipping role: a new emphasis on cargo carrying. By 1949 the group's cargo fleet had returned to its pre-war level – 245 ships, totalling 1.1 million tons. In 1939, the group had had 121 passenger ships, also totalling 1.1 million tons; 10 years later, there were only 70, and as their average size was little larger than before, this gave a total of only 660,000 tons. And as cargo ships were strengthened at the expense of passenger ships, changes in type came as well. The first – and in the proprietors' view, the most doubtful – was P&O's introduction to tankers. Ships needed oil; so did cars, motorcycles and aircraft; oil required purpose-built vessels to transport it. The company's annual report for 1955 stated the matter:

> It is for increased tanker tonnage more than for increased dry cargo tonnage that the world has been asking, and since at present the P&O Group neither owns nor operates any tankers, the Directors ... decided during the year to enter the tanker field, and berths have been reserved for some 500,000 tons d.w. of tankers for delivery during 1958, 1959 and 1960 from British shipyards.

The principle seemed sound, but by the spring of 1958, when P&O's

own tankers were just turning into physical realities, the tanker market collapsed. At that time, worldwide, there were more than 4 million dead weight tons of tankers laid up through lack of work. Nevertheless, the directors remained confident that tankers would prove a good investment in the long run, and the programme took a new tack: it looked as though, rather than a lot of small vessels, the market would need fewer but larger. The original group programme of 1955 divided half a million dead weight tons between 25 ships, an average of 20,000 tons a ship. By 1959 – with eight million surplus tons of tankers worldwide – P&O had modified its plan, maintaining the tonnage target, but dividing it between 14 ships, an average of over 35,000 tons a ship. A new company, Trident Tankers, was formed in 1962 to manage and operate all the group's tankers, and by 1964 Trident dominated the independent UK fleets: out of a national total of 7.47 million grt, Trident ran 2.4 million. In Britain, if one excluded the fleets of the oil majors, one tanker in every three was a P&O ship.

Even with this new and expensive venture, however, passenger shipping was not forgotten. Shortly after the tanker announcement of 1955 came news that two large 27-knot passenger ships would be

(Overleaf)
Orient Line was well known for the artistic standards it set, not merely in ship design but also in its publicity material. The merger with P&O's passenger operations in 1960 brought a new identity 'P&O – Orient Lines', into brief existence, but the confusing hybrid title was abandoned after only six years.

(Below)
When in the 1950s P&O entered the tanker trades, it began with ships of about 20,000 tons, but successive orders were for larger vessels. The 66,048-ton *Orissa* was built for Trident Tankers in 1965, but by 1970 215,000-ton tankers were in service.

RUN AWAY TO SEA
BY
P&O-ORIENT
LINES

Europe · Australia · New Zealand · Far East · Pacific · U.S.A · Canada

delivered for the Australian service in 1960. One, for the Orient Line, would be of 40,000 tons; she would be named *Oriana*, and would carry 2,050 passengers. The second ship's name was not at once revealed, and the directors were remarkably cryptic about her: all they would say was that she would be still larger, at 45,000 tons; that she would carry 2,250 passengers; and that her design would be 'unorthodox, with propelling machinery placed aft'.

On 3 November 1959, HRH Princess Alexandra launched *Oriana*, and on 16 March 1960 Dame Pattie Menzies launched P&O's 'unorthodox' passenger ship: *Canberra*. Both vessels were slightly larger than originally suggested, with *Oriana* at 42,000 and *Canberra* at 45,500 tons. Both were unusually stylish – more than a quarter of century later, *Canberra* is still a strikingly beautiful ship. And both were intended for use in a part of the world new to P&O – the Pacific. The Orient Line had first extended occasional voyages across the Pacific from Australia to Vancouver and San Francisco in 1954, a service which grew steadily and was augmented in 1958 by P&O's third *Himalaya*. Early in 1960, P&O, which already controlled Orient, offered to buy the balance of the company, and in May the name P&O-Orient Lines was given to the two companies' merged operations. Route maps showed the change in dramatic fashion: from Britain, through the Mediterranean and Suez to India, the Far East and Australia; on across the Pacific, up and down the West Coast of America, through the Panama Canal to the Atlantic, and back to Britain. As a whole, the group network had been established for decades, but now P&O itself encircled the world.

Oriana (41,900 tons) was delivered in November 1960, by which time P&O and Orient Line's passenger services had been merged. She carried 2,050 passengers on line voyages to Australia and the Pacific. As with ships as far back as *Viceroy of India*, much emphasis was placed on recreational facilities for travellers.

(*Above*)
Canberra, delivered to P&O in May 1961, was technically advanced whereas *Oriana* was conventional. The P&O ship was larger (45,000 tons), with space for 2,250 passengers, and cost £16 million; her maiden voyage was to the Pacific via Australia and back.

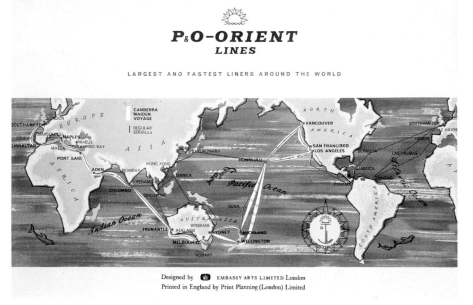

(*Left*)
Map of P&O-Orient Lines routes, 1961. One might have expected *Oriana* and *Canberra* to circumnavigate the world on their maiden voyages, but in fact they went out eastwards to Australia, crossed the Pacific – and returned by the way they came.

In 1963, a survey of world shipping trends since the beginning of the war was to reveal the extent of Britain's relative decline. British tonnage had increased by nearly a quarter, from 16.9 to over 20.3 million tons; yet world tonnage had doubled, from 61 to 121 million tons. The same survey showed how radically, within those figures, the face of British shipping had changed: dry-cargo tonnage under the Red Ensign had gone down by more than a million tons, and the increase in UK tonnage was entirely composed of tankers. And for its part – in spite of being a major owner and operator of UK-registered tankers – P&O had not stopped there. Air transport was taking passenger trades, and so, after more than a century as a shipping company, P&O had taken to the air.

In 1954, the group acquired a 70 per cent interest in Britavia Ltd, a company engaged in troop-carrying, with a fleet of four-engined Hermes aircraft. Britavia also had two wholly owned air subsidiaries, Silver City and Aquila, and, through the funds provided by P&O, its own airport, Ferryfield, in Kent. From there Silver City took motorists across the Channel to Le Touquet, and from a Scottish airport to Northern Ireland. Aquila was a flying-boat company – the only one in Britain – taking holidaymakers from Southampton to Madeira, Capri, Genoa and the Italian Riviera. In case it all seemed too much of a leap for the proprietors, Currie was careful to remind them that 'certain

P&O acquired a controlling interest in three small airlines in 1954, one of them being Silver City Airways which took motorists across the Channel from their airport at Ferryfield in Kent to Le Touquet in France in their Bristol Freighter aircraft.

companies in the Group were interesting themselves in air many years ago'. Orient Line, part of the group since 1919, had been involved in lighter-than-air developments in the late 1920s, and from the early 1930s had had a substantial interest in Imperial Airways. With Union Steam, they had been original shareholders in Australian National Airways; Union Steam itself founded and pioneered Union Airways of New Zealand, which in turn had a large stake in Tasman Empire Airways. Currie also emphasized that none of the group's new air companies was likely to be immediately profitable: 'They are long-term investments. We believe that they are of considerable potential value to the company, but they have a long way to go yet, and many obstacles must be overcome . . .'

The major possible obstacles were Government interference and limitation, but the commercial basis was already strong: in its previous trading year, Britavia had carried 91,000 passengers, 21,700 cars and over 8,000 motorcycles. Despite the radical nature of the move, the proprietors supported it. It was exciting and modern – air travel was the emblem of the age – and yet familiar. P&O had always been a transport company and only the element was different. Indeed, the proprietors became very keen on modernity, though as P&O's interest in air transport grew alongside its tanker fleet, Sir William Currie felt in 1958 that they needed to be actively dissuaded from the most modern navigational development of all – nuclear power.

P&O has usually been conservative with its ships. Only four in its history can be considered technically advanced: *Don Juan*, wrecked in 1837; the first *Himalaya*, a commercial failure; *Viceroy of India*, a magnificent success; and *Canberra*, doubted by many at first, but ultimately a success to compare with *Viceroy*. Currie's conservative remarks about nuclear ships were timely. *Savannah* – admittedly built for demonstration only – was never a success and is now a museum ship in Charleston, South Carolina, USA, and apart from icebreakers her successors have had no more success.

The changes and developments within shipping and outside it were innovative, forward-looking, even adventurous; and had they been the only events to affect P&O in the 1950s, the company's story would have been smooth, calm and eternally optimistic. But it was never smooth or calm, and sometimes it was deeply pessimistic. For outside the control of Chairman or directors was a series of events – natural, political and commercial – which were effectively anti-shipping.

After the war, as proprietors dreamed of a return to pre-war normality, 1949 gave shape to the new kind of normality P&O had to face. The communists' victory in the Chinese civil war cut off trade there almost completely, and shook Hong Kong – as Currie noted, 'even being an island does not insulate a territory against the ferments of its mainland'. The separation of the Indian and Pakistani economies, when their rulers disagreed on whether or not to devalue, created vast problems for BI; and in Australia, East Africa and the Persian Gulf there were strikes and congestion in ports, at a time when it cost more than £2,000 a day to keep a *Strath* vessel in port, and over £2,300 if she was delayed with passengers. And no less ominously for Far Eastern operations, Sir William Currie warned the proprietors that 'Japanese shipping, which before the war was an important factor in world trade, is on its way back'.

The 1930s had been bad and the 1940s worse, but throughout there had been the assumption that time and work would improve matters. The 1950s opened with war in Korea and in Indo-China, with a national emergency in Malaya, with high inflation, go-slows and strikes, with ship turn-arounds in Australian ports taking 45 days instead of 14; and

Strathnaver in London Docks towards the end of her life. Until the advent of containers in the late 1960s, P&O's passenger liners continued to rely on their cargo holds for a substantial amount of revenue.

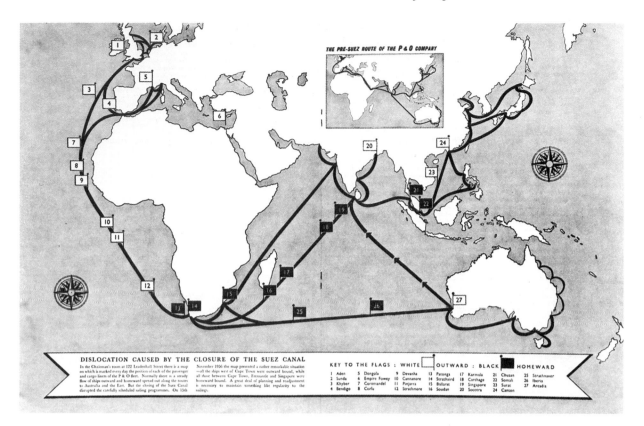

THE PRE-SUEZ ROUTE OF THE P & O COMPANY

DISLOCATION CAUSED BY THE CLOSURE OF THE SUEZ CANAL

In the Chairman's room at 122 Leadenhall Street there is a map on which is marked every day the position of each of the passenger and cargo liners of the P & O fleet. Normally there is a steady flow of ships outward and homeward spread out along the routes to Australia and the East. But the closing of the Suez Canal disrupted the carefully scheduled sailing programmes. On 15th

November 1956 the map presented a rather remarkable situation —all the ships west of Cape Town were outward bound, while all those between Cape Town, Fremantle and Singapore were homeward bound. A great deal of planning and readjustment is necessary to maintain something like regularity to the sailings.

KEY TO THE FLAGS : WHITE ☐ OUTWARD : BLACK ■ HOMEWARD

1	Aden	5	Dongola	9	Devanha	13	Patonga	17	Karmala	21	Chusan	25	Strathnaver
2	Sunda	6	Empire Fowey	10	Cannanore	14	Strathaird	18	Carthage	22	Somali	26	Iberia
3	Khyber	7	Coromandel	11	Pinjarra	15	Ballarat	19	Singapore	23	Surat	27	Arcadia
4	Bendigo	8	Corfu	12	Strathmore	16	Soudan	20	Socotra	24	Canton		

for once Currie began to feel things might not get better at all. 'The future', he observed, 'is indeed cloudy, with scarcely a streak of blue.... We must be prepared to have more competition, in the main from our former enemies, Japan, Germany and Italy. What an extraordinary thing modern civilization is; we fight ourselves into bankruptcy to defeat the enemy, and now the enemy is gradually getting back into the saddle and into its old trades.' And, he might have added, with a good deal of guidance – in the case of Japan – from the old ally, America. He could be forgiven his apparent despondency; the world had become a disheartening place, and he was beginning to grow old.

But the discouragement, legitimate as it was, was a passing mood. A shipping company which had weathered every discouragement since the sinking of its first mail-carrying ship on its first mail-carrying voyage was not going to let itself founder on changing patterns of trade. And a chairman who had led the company through history's most destructive war was not going to be defeated by peace. Sir William took P&O into new fields, the tanker trade and aviation, and tantalized people with the company's plans for *Canberra*. However, not even he could have forecast the next hurdle. For as he himself remarked, 'Who would have thought... that a few months later the greatest international shipping highway in the world would be blocked?'

The seizure of the Suez Canal Company by Egypt on 26 July 1956, and the blocking of the Canal in November, had an immediate effect on P&O. The Canal was the keystone to most of the company's operations between Europe, Australia and the East, and its closure made a dramatic

Map showing the positions of the 27 P&O ships at the closure of the Suez Canal in November 1956. The disruption caused by this action can well be envisaged, though by the time the Canal was shut again eleven years later the company was able to adapt much more easily.

hiatus in carefully planned routes and timetables. Recently, company reports had become illustrated with photographs of the group's ships and activities – an effective addition to good communications – and one picture from 1956 proudly showed BI's *Uganda* with P&O's *Iberia* at Capetown, both out of their usual waters after diversion from Suez. It was a further proof of the company's continuing flexibility and capacity for change; and although some parts of the group were badly hit by the closure, for a short while the group as a whole benefitted quite markedly. Before tax, group net profit for the year rose from £12.5 million to £17.6 million. But the stimulus given to shipping – from longer routes, higher rates, fears of war and brisk trading to ward off shortages – was brief. After the Canal's reopening in 1957, group ships began to pass through it again in May. At the end of the accounting year, pre-tax profits had fallen to £10.1 million – less than before the closure; and in October, P&O's cargo ship *Shillong* collided with the tanker *Purfina Congo* at night in the Gulf of Suez. *Shillong* sank with the loss of three lives – a final, unpleasant postscript to a episode which may have been profitable but which was badly disturbing as well.

Group troop ships were involved in the Suez campaign, as were Aquila's flying boats, but after the end of National Service in Britain most of the ships were no longer needed for Government contracts. In 1961, using their surplus troop ships, BI initiated a series of educational cruises for schoolchildren. These proved immediately and consistently popular, attracting about 37,000 children and 10,000 teachers or independent passengers annually. It was, in its way, the passengers' parallel of another psychological move taken in 1949. In that year, BI reintroduced a practice dropped during the war, and harking back to what people were rapidly beginning to think of as the good old days – the system of training their cadets in ships especially run for the purpose. Although P&O never adopted the system itself, the New Zealand Shipping Company also ran special cadet ships with at least as much enthusiasm and fervour as BI. And if it sounded archaic and unrealistic at first, it had a canny basis: 'this method', Currie explained, 'inculcates in these boys an *esprit de corps* and an atmosphere of tradition which is invaluable in later years.' It was a wise move, for as the real imperial tradition crumbled and competition became sharper and more varied, company loyalty would become more and more important for survival and growth.

Sir William Currie retired on 30 March 1960, at the age of 76. He was P&O Chairman for 22 years and connected with the company (through BI and Mackinnon's) since 1914. *Oriana* had been launched only 21 weeks and *Canberra* only two weeks before his retirement – a splendid swansong. It was good there was a high note on which he could end and retire with grace, for otherwise his departure could have been painful for all concerned. Feeling in the company towards him was unanimous but paradoxical: he was highly respected and well-liked – indeed, loved – for his personal appreciation of all employees. 'He could meet you in the street,' wrote one, 'remember your Christian name, and leave an impression of warm humanity and strength, which not only endeared him to you but won your life-long loyalty.' There was no pretence in his warmth; that was the way he was. And because of that, as he grew older, slower, and less able to make the swift decisions his juniors believed essential, so it became more difficult for anyone to point out that he really ought to retire.

Sir Donald Anderson was his obvious and intended successor. Born in 1906, he joined the family firm, Anderson Green and Company – managers of the Orient Line – in 1928, transferred to P&O in 1934 and was appointed an Assistant Manager two years later. In 1950 he became Deputy Chairman, and after being knighted in 1954, it was he who initiated P&O's programme of tanker building in 1955. Currie was already over 70 and could reasonably be expected to retire soon but the idea did not occur to him at all. It was not that he was hanging on to power grimly, in the face of opposition; it was simply that shipping, and particularly P&O, was his life. Several previous chairmen had gone on longer than he, even – like the first Lord Inchcape – remaining until they dropped dead in office; and if he gave it thought, that was probably how he imagined his own end. But it did not help the company, and eventually, when Sir Donald was offered the chairmanship of a major clearing bank, the time came for a decision.

To minimize embarrassment and give Currie time to absorb the matter, Anderson went on holiday and wrote to him, asking his plans for retirement and pointing out that he, Anderson, was still young enough to do something else.

Currie did retire, and without acrimony: his final Chairman's Address was as warm towards Anderson as anything he had ever said or done. Nevertheless, Sir Donald did not have an easy start.

12

CHANGING PATTERNS

There were some striking contrasts between the outgoing Chairman and his successor. Currie, never a very big man, had become stooped with age, while over the years his genial nature brought an avuncular, even a grandfatherly, aspect to his chairmanship. When Sir Donald Anderson took charge, however, he took full control as well. Physically, he was an imposing presence, patrician in appearance and manner. In character, he was clear-headed, decisive, impatient of the second-rate. In many ways he was a natural leader and everyone who encountered him soon came to respect him highly, but to those who did not know him well, he could be a daunting and frightening man, seemingly distant and autocratic. Yet even those who missed the warmth of Sir William's time had no hesitation in acknowledging the urgent need for powerful leadership, for 'when misfortune comes to shipping, it comes as an epidemic'.

With those words Anderson began his second annual address as Chairman in 1962. 'We have to look back to the 1930s to seek a parallel to conditions today,' he continued, 'and even there we shall not find it.' Since 1957, the group's pre-tax profits had taken a nosedive: from the

Sir Donald Forsyth Anderson (1906–1973), who succeeded Sir William Currie as P&O Chairman in 1960 after ten years as Deputy Chairman.
(Oil by Derek Hill, 1970)

£17.6 million of 1957 down to £10.1 million, plunging to £4.6 million in 1959, slightly back in 1960 to £5.8 million, and then in 1961 almost vanishing altogether – less than £600,000. But unlike the slump of the 1930s, that of the early 1960s was not general; it was confined to shipping because there were simply too many ships in the world for the available demand. And the major cause of that was the astonishing rise in ships registered under flags of convenience, the flags of countries – particularly Liberia and Panama – whose taxes were lower than those of the shipowner's own country. Giving 1939 an index figure of 100, Sir Donald reported that at the end of 1961, British shipping stood at 93, America at 94, Japan at 109 – and Panama at 700.

'We have sold ships; we have laid up ships; we have withdrawn altogether from certain trades...' P&O's investment in air transport had been short-lived: by the end of the 1950s the operating companies had been closed or sold, and the company became merely a minority shareholder in British United Airways. The group had also reduced turn-round times for its ships, cut costs at sea and on shore, intensified competition and in some trades cooperated with other owners to reduce the number of ships needed. Everything possible was being done; and it was pleasing that 'but for the tankers, our results would have been even worse'. They were paying their way and so were *Oriana* and *Canberra*.

'They have no equal in their trades,' Sir Donald said of them, 'and we

Oriana was the last passenger liner built to carry Orient Line's distinctive 'corn' hull colours, introduced in 1935. In the interests of uniformity they gave way to P&O white in the mid 1960s, though a similar colour was revived for P&O cargo ships a decade later.

believe they are likely to make the best of the conditions they have to meet, good or bad.' They were not invulnerable, though. In December 1962, *Oriana* collided with the American aircraft carrier *USS Kearsage* off Long Beach, California; and on 4 January 1963, *Canberra* hit the headlines – 'Fire Cripples P&O Liner'.

'Fire struck the 45,000-ton liner *Canberra*, flagship of the P&O-Orient Lines fleet, as she steamed eastwards off the southern tip of Italy,' *The Times* recorded. 'The main engines were put out of action and the £16m liner – Britain's biggest to be built since the Queen Elizabeth – came to a standstill.'

Stratheden, homeward bound from Australia, was soon alongside, and happily, none of *Canberra*'s 2,222 passengers was injured. The fire had begun in the main engine room switchboard, and took almost an hour to control. Naturally publicity was immense but to Sir Donald's relief, 'a great many passengers' from *Canberra* said that 'their opinion of the company has been increased – not diminished – by the way in which the whole affair was handled.' Since few people needed to travel by sea any more, they had to be persuaded; and what could have been a tragedy became something of a benefit to public relations.

There had been little by way of good public relations, and a great deal of tragedy, in the loss of the BI passenger/cargo liner *Dara* nearly two years earlier. On 7 April 1961 she was unloading cargo and disembarking passengers at Dubai when a violent storm made it necessary to leave harbour and ride out the gale off shore. While returning to Dubai at 4.40 a.m. the following day an explosion between decks was followed by fire. A certain amount of panic among crew and passengers caused several lifeboats to capsize, and though British, German and Norwegian vessels were on hand, 238 passengers, crew and Dubai shore staff died out of a complement of 819. The fire was controlled by naval parties and *Dara* was taken under tow, but she sank five kilometres off Dubai at 9.20 a.m. on 10 April 1961. It was later thought that the explosion was caused by a terrorist device, but concrete proof was not forthcoming.

In 1962, the group made a pre-tax loss of £61,000; and the following year came *Canberra*'s near-disaster. Inevitably, the great passenger liner herself lost money but in spite of that, for the year 1963 as a whole, it almost seemed as if any publicity was good. The group made a pre-tax profit again, back up at £4.2 million, and if, as Sir Donald acknowledged, it was 'a very small return on the £170 million' invested, at least a corner appeared to have been turned.

In 1963 there came two more valuable cargo initiatives. The first was the decision to order four 40,000-ton bulk carriers which were delivered in 1965; the second was to enter into a long-term agreement with the Anglo Norness Shipping Company, one of the world's foremost operators of tankers and bulk carriers. Under this agreement, P&O and Anglo Norness established Associated Bulk Carriers, a joint company based in Bermuda, to market their fleets of bulk carriers and oil/bulk/ore carriers. Tankers were growing ever larger: P&O's first, delivered in 1958, had been less than 20,000 tons, yet only six years later, at the end of 1964, *Ottawa* was delivered – 89,000 dead weight tons. Bulk carriers transformed the dry-cargo trade in a similar way,

Divers on the wreck of *Dara* recovered the trigger guard and magazine from a Mauser carbine. This did not prove sabotage, but somebody aboard was evidently smuggling arms in their luggage.

through simple economies of size.

The year 1963 offered a bit of luck as well. Grain harvests in Russia and China were bad and the resulting vast purchases of grain from the West gave a much-needed fillip to the freight industry generally. But there were also two bad omens for British shipping and shipbuilding. In a way which Sir Donald called 'extraordinarily self-centred', the United States began trying to regulate the international liner shipping industry – 'Washington DC', the Chairman remarked, 'seems determined to assume control and to spread a thick layer of glue over what remains of the works.' Simultaneously, P&O had been able to order three of its bulk carriers in British yards but 'no UK yard could offer yet another ship on the same terms', and 'on both price and delivery date' the fourth ship went to Japan.

In 1965, the shipbuilding firm of Fairfield's collapsed as, in the face of foreign competition, the industry's agonizing contraction began. The P&O Group had had two ships under construction at Fairfield's, with a third ordered, for which a first instalment of £320,000 had been paid. Government intervention enabled the first two vessels to be built. As for the third, however, 'no work had been done on her, and it was clear that none would be'. P&O became an unsecured creditor, 'for what that is worth'. It was particularly galling that the ship, one of four oil/bulk/ore carriers on order for the group, could have been built much more cheaply in Japan. A bulk carrier was ordered there instead and gave some consolation by being delivered before the Fairfield's 'obo' had been expected in the first place, but still, as Sir Donald said, 'our gesture of goodwill towards British shipbuilding turned out to be very expensive for us, and of no help to the shipbuilding industry'.

1965 also brought three striking new ventures for the group. With Ranger Fishing, it entered the freezer-trawler business. Through

In 1965 P&O took delivery of its first bulk carriers, managed by Hain-Nourse Ltd, a merger of two existing Group companies. The ships were named after foxhunts at Sir Donald Anderson's suggestion, and here the first, the 43,965 dwt *Atherstone*, passes through the Panama Canal.

Sir Donald Anderson was convinced that containers were the way of the future, making general cargo handling a labour-saving and cost-intensive business, but it involved substantial investment in new ships, containers and shore facilities, only possible through involvement with other shipowners in the OCL partnership.

North Sea Ferries, an associate of General Steam, it bought its first roll-on/roll-off vehicle ferries. But most important, most costly and most ambitious of the new investments was the creation of Overseas Containers Ltd (OCL): container shipping was perhaps the most profound development in cargo liner trades since the change from sail to steam.

OCL was formed by four of the leading British independent shipping companies – P&O, Alfred Holt, British & Commonwealth, and Furness Withy. Their importance may be judged by the fact that, together, they operated 60 per cent of all British independently owned tankers. However, moving into containers was completely new for them all, with immense implications. Sir Andrew Crichton was seconded from the board of P&O to be founding chairman of OCL and mastermind of the huge changes involved. They did not mean simply a new method of packing cargoes; they meant working out the design and delivery of various types of container, building container bases and ship terminals, arranging new inland transport systems, planning and installing electronic data processing, changing traditional handling methods in the docks – indeed, completely reshaping a major section of the shipping industry. One did not have to think far ahead to realize Sir Donald Anderson was right when he warned that this 'revolutionary system of overseas transport' was 'bound to lead to very heavy obsolescence in ships, practices and ideas'.

The second half of the 1960s was the most turbulent five-year period the shipping world has ever experienced in peacetime. During 1966, in P&O's own estimate, 'the most important event of the year was the strike by the National Union of Seamen [NUS]'. Its root cause, in the company's view, was union greed. An agreement of the previous year, which had already increased British shipowners' crew costs by $14\frac{1}{2}$ per cent, was repudiated by the NUS. The strike began on 16 May, affecting every shipping company, and lasted until 1 July. For P&O, it meant the immobilization of five of the company's ships, the loss of £1.4 million, and a massive dislocation of voyage schedules – the last of the immobilized ships could not return to schedule until March 1967. Strikes were not just a British trend: another, lasting five weeks, took place in Montreal, along with stoppages in other Canadian ports. In Asia came an even more damaging political development: war between India and Pakistan. Normally served as one trade, they suddenly had to be split in two, 'with every sort of confusion and delay', while in Australia, disaster came from nature. A severe drought killed more than 10 million sheep in New South Wales alone. In each of the areas affected, the P&O group had a major or dominant interest, and as the Chairman remarked, 'the combination of these particular strokes of Fate might have been designed specifically for us. . . . We have all had a year we would like to forget.'

But, while the word 'Washington' began to vie with 'Greek' as a term of disgust in British shipowners' vocabulary, and though the time of slump and difficulty was not finished, the company had no intention of

(*Above*)
Containerisation can even be applied to giraffes, which the company first carried in 1836!

(*Left*)
The first class of OCL ships, six 29,000 tonners built for the Australian service in 1969–70, could each carry 1,900 twenty-foot containers and replaced four or five times as many general cargo ships.

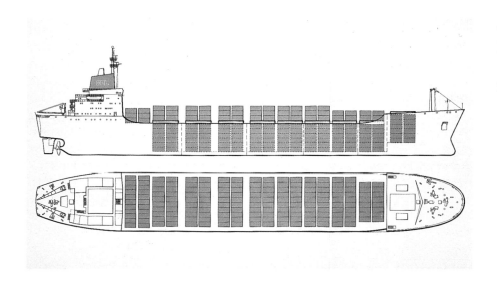

giving up its leading position or of ignoring new developments. The containers were coming and would change dockland completely. Instead of a labour-intensive business, loading and unloading ships would become a capital-intensive business: the expensive new system required far fewer workers than before.

For some, the prospect was invigorating; for others, threatening. Remaining optimistic, Anderson hoped 1967 would improve and help erase the memory of 1966. Yet if anything, it seemed worse. The company's financial year began with the aftermath of the seamen's strike and ended with serious dock strikes in Liverpool and London, as union leaders realized that containers would disrupt the working practices of generations of dockworkers. The future of the Panama Canal was under discussion between America and Panama, with the likelihood of greatly increased tolls. Egypt and Israel went to war; on 5 June the Suez Canal was closed again; and finally, in the autumn, the pound sterling was devalued.

The dock strikes cost P&O £$\frac{1}{2}$ million; and after two closures in 11 years, the Suez Canal had become completely unreliable. Nevertheless, neither the year nor the company's prospects were quite as gloomy when fully assessed. Profits had revived after the damage inflicted in 1966. The strikes of 1967 had sprung, paradoxically, from the ending of casual labour in the docks, and with guaranteed employment on one hand, greater productivity was anticipated on the other. As in 1956, the Suez closure forced a drastic revision of voyage plans – but 'at least none of the group ships was trapped.... We might have had *Canberra* with nearly 3,000 people on board sitting there now if she had not been turned back 24 hours short of Port Said'.

More importantly, that experience taught shipowners to reduce dependence on the waterway. 'Shipping can live with the Canal open, and it can live with the Canal shut. What it cannot live with is a Canal that may at any moment upset the always uneasy equilibrium between supply and demand in world shipping.' Passenger shipping would remain vulnerable – but not tankers: they were already becoming too large to use Suez. P&O shareholders – initially very wary of tankers – began to thank their lucky stars that the directors had been so determined to move into that market.

Even devaluation turned out to be a net benefit for the group: sterling revenue from existing dollar contracts increased, while it became possible to quote keener rates than before for new non-sterling business. In 1968, assessing the group's tankers and looking forward to the delivery of OCL's container ships, Sir Donald commented that it was always the same with new methods: 'They are first considered laughable, then objectionable, and finally obvious.' Despite the very painful transition, he remained certain that containers were the way of the future, just as tankers had proved to be.

Whenever possible, P&O had always been careful to arrange long-term charters for its tankers, to avoid the fluctuations of voyage charter rates. Indeed, some of its tankers were ordered for specific oil-company charters and were sold once those charters expired. However, in spite of this prudence, there was no chance for the company to rest on its laurels

or become complacent. In April 1968 the new ferry *Wahine*, belonging to the Union Steamship Company of New Zealand, grounded in an extremely severe freak storm at the entrance to Wellington harbour. Fifty-one people died but a court of inquiry established that no one – neither captain, owners, nor anyone else – was to blame. Nevertheless, the tragic accident underlined that even in a perfectly ordered system, acts of God could intrude. And there seemed no end to the intrusive acts of man. Communist state-owned merchant ships began what amounted to a politically inspired trade offensive, still continuing, by undercutting typical Western freight rates by 15 per cent – competition which was impossible to match commercially. By 1969, the UK coffee-carrying trade had been lost to Communist shipping. Furthermore, the unpo-

Silley, Cox & Company, a P&O subsidiary from the First World War until the 1970s, were shiprepairers at Falmouth, an ideal location for such a trade. They undertook work for Group companies when appropriate, but got most of their business from outside concerns.

The Group's last passenger liner operating between Britain and East Africa, BI's *Kenya* (14,434 grt), built for the route in 1951, is seen here at Durban. She was sold for scrap after the service had been killed by the closure of the Suez Canal and the growth of jet aircraft.

pular, distressing but essential transition to container carrying was not over – although it was by no means the only reason for the abnormally bad national and international industrial relations of the period. In Falmouth, Silley, Cox & Company (one of the group's subsidiaries) owned four dry docks, including one of the largest privately owned ones in the country – the Queen Elizabeth Dock, capable of taking tankers of over 85,000 tons. During the early months of the year, a national engineering strike was threatened. The mere threat hit Silley, Cox badly, causing worried shipowners to keep their vessels away from UK yards. Meanwhile, the Transport and General Workers' Union blacked the group's developing container terminal at Tilbury; in distant Colombo and Trincomalee, there were frequent labour disputes; in Auckland, seamen went on strike for 52 days, immobilizing 17 Union Company vessels; and along the east coast of America and the Gulf of Mexico, stevedores also went on strike for three months.

The strikes were commercially hurtful but commercial sense dictated changes which, for sentimental reasons, were more hurtful still. P&O had already sold its major Indian interests – the Bombay and Calcutta ship-repair yards and the pilgrim-carrying Mogul Line – in 1960. In

1969, the continued closure of the Suez Canal meant that, after well over a century of constant links, P&O was obliged to withdraw its regular passenger services to the Far East. Similarly, BI had already lost its Indian coasting trade and, in 1957, moved its management to London. In June 1969 BI's *Kenya* was sold – the group's last passenger ship operating between the UK and East Africa. With the sale of *Rangitoto* that year, 96 years of passenger service by the New Zealand Shipping Company ended; and early in 1970, with *Chusan*, outward bound, P&O ran its last Indian passenger sailing.

An outbreak of typhoid in *Oronsay* knocked a swift £500,000 off estimated profits for P&O's other passenger services and the advent of jumbo jets threatened their final erosion. By then, the group owned 266 vessels either in existence or building, and was involved in almost every kind of shipping except icebreakers. Group ships ranged from trawlers to chemical carriers and only 21 of them were passenger vessels. Yet, there was no thought of withdrawing altogether from passenger shipping; apart from the sheer level of investment, the fame of the ships and P&O's traditional high standard of service in them provided a first-rate shop window to the world. Now, in 1969, P&O began to extend its own cruising operations to the potentially lucrative market of America's West Coast.

But one of the most important and positive shipping events of that important year took place on 6 March. On that day, OCL's *Encounter Bay* began her maiden voyage, inaugurating the first fully cellular container service in the UK/Continental/Australia trade. It marked the end of ten full years of Anderson's chairmanship of the group and four

'Alaska Ahoy!' In 1969 P&O extended its cruising operations by introducing voyages out of San Francisco. Here *Arcadia* (29,664 grt, built 1954) braves the icy waters of the Alaskan coast. The expectations of the North American market prompted P&O to invest in purpose-built cruise ships from 1972 onwards.

The new P&O Building in Leadenhall Street, completed in 1969, was as modern as the old office had been out of date. The company only stayed in residence for ten years, after 117 years in '122'.

years of Sir Andrew Crichton's chairmanship of OCL – and, they both devoutly hoped, the beginning of a period of trading that could be profitable, and peaceful as well.

Anderson hoped for peaceful profits not only for the sake of the company but also because he was preparing to retire – one of his early alterations of management rules was to ensure that all non-executive directors would retire at 70, and executive directors at 65. Thus it was all the more disappointing for him personally when, late in 1970, he made his penultimate statement to shareholders: 'I did not foresee the range of troubles that would plague OCL during its first year of operations,' he admitted frankly, 'nor the resulting loss. . . . Accumulated losses amounted to over £9 million by the end of September 1970, and will probably amount to some £13–14 million by September 1971.'

The OCL losses were serious, yet Anderson remained convinced that containers were the transport system of the future and noted that operating losses had been made not by the container ships themselves but by the remaining conventional shipping in OCL. There were many other mitigating factors too: for example, appalling delays in the delivery of ships – P&O's first liquefied petroleum gas carrier, due for delivery in October 1970, would not now come into service until early 1972; its successor, intended for May 1971, would not now be ready until December 1972. As the British shipbuilding industry continued to shrink, Cammell Laird's yard entered financial crisis. Four P&O contracts there had to be cancelled and transferred to Norway, entailing the loss of a year's trading with them. And on 21 September 1970, the Devlin Report Stage II came into effect in a way which 'so far ... can only be called disastrous'. The report completed the process of 'decasualization' of dock labour, and Anderson approved of the principle involved; he called it 'a revolution in the terms of employment

Gazana, P&O's first liquefied petroleum gas carrier, with a capacity of some 29,000 cubic metres, enters the water at Cammell Laird's Birkenhead yard on 24 May 1971

P&O Offshore Services was formed in 1964 to service gas and later oil rigs. Here the supply vessel *Lady Margaret* attends the exploration rig *Sea Quest* in the North Sea. Six years later P&O joined with four American partners in the search for North Sea oil of their own.

in the docks, which has substituted security for casual employment, self respect for a feeling of neglect, and a very high fixed hourly wage for the inequities of piece work'. But he was bitter about the result – a drop in productivity of 'at least 20 per cent on exports and $33\frac{1}{3}$ per cent on imports'. Worse still, loading costs for exports had risen by 25–30 per cent, and discharging costs for imports by at least 60 per cent, and sometimes as much as 70 per cent.

Beset by these problems, P&O gambled on entering an ultra-modern non-shipping field, though the involvement came about through shipping. P&O Offshore Services had been formed in 1964 to make use of an enormous opportunity – offshore oil and gas. It began with six specialized craft for servicing gas rigs in the southern North Sea. This extended later to other parts of the world, and to the servicing of oil rigs. From there, Sir Donald Anderson was able to report in 1970 on a new, intensely exciting prospect – and prospect was exactly the right word. Recalling that he had joined P&O in 1934 after six years with Orient Line, he remarked that 'except for the names and house flags, in no other way does the group even faintly resemble the organization I joined'. Now there were more than 100 companies in the group, employing 40,000 people all round the world. Anderson acknowledged that, for P&O, its new venture was a development unlike anything it had ever done before, but 'it has become clear that oil fields of major magnitude exist under the North Sea Continental Shelf.' In June 1970,

P&O had joined with four American oil companies to search for the North Sea's treasure. 'High risk', said Sir Donald drily, 'and, potentially, high return.'

Despite this announcement P&O had no intention of deserting shipping altogether, and in February 1971 announced the takeover of the Coast Lines group of ferry, short-sea cargo and road transport companies for £5.6 million in P&O deferred stock. Coast Lines' shipping services concentrated on the Irish Sea and the North of Scotland, and therefore fitted in well beside those of General Steam; the haulage companies enlarged the Group's fleet to some 6,000 load-carrying units, about a quarter being tankers, operating in the UK, Ireland and Continental Europe.

During the second half of the 1960s, despite the terrible difficulties of those years, group pre-tax profits had risen from £4 million in 1966 to £12.6 million in 1969. To build it up to that point against the odds was a considerable achievement but in 1971, the year of Sir Donald's retirement, the auditors reported a staggering fall to £4.9 million – in real terms, the lowest figure for five years.

Two main items brought about the sorry results: a rapid escalation in operating costs, and a dramatic decline in dry-cargo freight rates. A ship of 40,000 tons or more had been able to charge $5.15 per dead weight ton per month in 1970; in 1971, the same ship could only charge $1.35. Perhaps Anderson was disappointed to be leaving his life-time group at such a moment; yet perhaps he left with some relief as well. It had been a hard battle, and, with good ideas taking longer than expected to prove worthwhile and old trades changing or dying out, at times it may have seemed a losing battle as well. He handed over to his successor, Ford Geddes, in the autumn of 1971, confident that all would soon be well. But in fact, P&O was on the brink of one of the worst crises it had faced in all its peacetime existence.

13

LOCAL WARS

Ford Geddes and Sir Donald Anderson were second cousins, and both rose through the family firm, Anderson Green; Geddes joined it in 1934, the same year Anderson transferred to P&O, and in 1960, when P&O-Orient was created, Geddes joined the P&O board. During the strike of the National Union of Seamen in 1966, he led the shipowners' side of the negotiations, and was publicly praised by Sir Donald for his dignity, firmness, coolness, reason and lack of animosity in handling a critical dispute.

As an executive director, Geddes considered he had already reached his personal pinnacle in the P&O hierarchy, and was contemplating early retirement when Sir Donald indicated that he would probably become the next Chairman. It was irresistible – 'the proudest moment of my life', Geddes said later.

A modest man with a strong sense of duty, he had recently persuaded Anderson to engage the management consultants McKinsey to advise on P&O's cumbersome management structure. The group as a whole included 127 different companies, each with varying degrees of answerability to the main Board, while 23 people reported directly to the Chairman. Various uncomplimentary terms – feudal, Victorian, autocratic – could be, and were, applied to this system but more after Sir Donald's retirement than when he was in control, for it was a system which had suited him, and which he had suited in return.

The McKinsey reorganization of P&O was a radical and thorough operation. A precursor had taken place in 1960, when P&O and Orient merged their shipping management. The rather clumsy name P&O-Orient had been coined to try and distinguish between P&O as a shipping company in its own right, and P&O as parent of a group of other shipping companies. In 1966, the 'Orient' half of the name was dropped, and ever since, it had become clear that the attempted distinction between P&O and the group's other companies was increasingly artificial, and a handicap to full efficiency. For example, P&O, BI and Eastern & Australian – a member of the group since 1946 – all operated passenger ships; P&O, BI, New Zealand Shipping and others in the group all operated cargo liners. So, instead of having so many different, overlapping companies within the group, it was decided to alter the whole company structure on to a divisional basis. There would be only five main divisions: bulk shipping; general cargo shipping; passenger shipping; European and air transport; and 'general holdings'.

'It will be clear', said Sir Donald in his explanation of the change, 'that the new divisions are large and very important commercial and ship management enterprises.' Inevitably, there were many sad disap-

pearances; the shipping companies were most affected, with traditional
company names, flags and liveries vanishing. Hain's and Nourse Line
had already been joined as Hain-Nourse to look after the Group's bulk
carriers; now the names went completely, to become part of the Bulk
Shipping Division. The New Zealand Shipping Company had recently
ceased to be shipowners and became P&O (NZ) Ltd; British India, one
of the proudest of all shipping names, became simply a tradename for
educational cruises; General Steam disappeared into the European and
Air Transport Division. Many of the old companies remained as
registered owners of ships but became 'invisible' to the general public;
where there had been many flags, an outside observer now saw only
P&O.

The change, unsettling as it was for those who cherished their
particular traditions, made eminent commercial sense. But, of course, it

could not be done overnight. 'A reorganization of this magnitude must be carefully planned,' said Sir Donald, 'and implemented gradually, if present operations are not to suffer.... We must continue to make a success of the old system while planning the details of the new, and indeed until the new system is ready to take over.'

Yet in spite of the initiative, the sense and the preparation, by April 1972 – eight months after he had become Chairman – Ford Geddes was faced by discouraging preliminary figures for the company's financial year: it looked as though the low profit of the year before would be repeated, or worse. Simultaneously, the property market was booming. In P&O's £400 million gross assets, its properties were listed as representing only £27.5 million, but their true value was £100 million, and rising. When published in the next accounts, the written-up figures would make the group's paltry predicted earnings appear still worse. At the time Geddes had come to the chair, P&O's rival Cunard was taken

In the early 1970s the new divisional structure meant a loss of identity for most of P&O's shipowning subsidiaries. For the bulk and general cargo ships – the overwhelming majority of the fleet – this was epitomized by the introduction of new Group funnel colours bearing a P&O logo.

In the past P&O had tended
to treat its properties as
merely tools of its operations,
but realized in the early
1970s that its buildings (such
as the P&O Building in
Sydney) were much more
valuable as investments in
their own right.

over by Trafalgar House, and now Geddes warned his staff that even P&O was 'not necessarily too large to be the subject of a bid'.

The property boom affected the housebuilding and construction company Bovis even more. Its profits had risen from £¾ million in 1967 to a predicted £13 million for 1972. At the end of May, when the Chairman of Lazard's merchant bank, Lord Poole, joined the Board of P&O, Geddes and his colleagues were already considering the possibility of group diversification into leisure, transport or construction. As it happened, Lazard's also worked for Bovis; Bovis was looking for a union with a larger company. Lord Poole saw a way to make everyone happy.

Late in June, Geddes and Bovis Chairman Frank Sanderson met. On 10 August the result of the talks between the two was published: an agreed bid by P&O for Bovis, valuing Bovis at £130 million. It was rather reminiscent of that other historic, secretly negotiated union back in 1914, when Thomas Sutherland and the first Lord Inchcape brought P&O and British India together. Beyond that, another practical similarity was that, in the same way as the first Lord Inchcape had promptly become Sutherland's successor-designate, it seemed that so too would Sanderson to Geddes. One of the first agreements was that he would enter P&O as Joint Deputy Chairman of the enlarged group, and as Chairman of an executive committee, recommended by McKinsey's as the proper way of running the group day to day. From there it would probably only be a question of time before Sanderson inherited the chair of the entire P&O group. In the past it had been said that if P&O had acquired the shares of British India, Inchcape had acquired P&O. Now it looked as though P&O would acquire the shares of Bovis, and Sanderson would acquire P&O.

Perhaps it would have worked. Not many years before, the proprietors of P&O – or any company's shareholders – would have had little real say in such matters. Most would have been content to trust their directors and would have accepted the enlargement without question. Instead, the announcement of 10 August set in motion one hundred of the most dramatic days either P&O or the City had ever seen, culminating in the resignation of Ford Geddes and six other P&O directors.

The deal had already come close to being called off, when the two companies' merchant bankers could not agree on terms. However, an agreement was worked out– an agreement later described as 'a hotch-potch package, almost impossible to value'. And that difficulty of valuation was the key to the violent, unhappy hundred days which followed.

At first all seemed quite smooth, so much so that Geddes went on holiday the day after the bid was announced, and Sanderson looked forward to his own holiday in a fortnight's time. But on 13 August a brief note in a national newspaper indicated that the third Lord Inchcape, a non-executive director of P&O since 1951, was unsure about the bid. On 24 August, having had two weeks to think about it, a fortnightly magazine, *Investors' Review*, published its own analysis, with the uncompromising conclusion that P&O shareholders should reject the deal.

The initiative of opposition had been taken, simultaneously and separately, by two people. One was a journalist who assessed the deal as a drastic devaluation of P&O's asset backing per share, with the benefit going to Bovis shareholders. The other was a P&O shareholder, a suburban investment manager who reckoned building was due for a downturn and shipping for an upturn, who had just switched £$\frac{1}{2}$ million out of building and into shipping, and who did not want to see his own judgment overridden unilaterally. Inchcape suddenly realized that others shared his misgivings and burst into equally categorical print three days later; buying Bovis, he said, would be in 'the worst interests of P&O shareholders'.

The fat was thrown accurately into the fire and blazed up at once. Today, if a takeover bid is under way, it is no novelty to see large, expensive advertisements in the national press with the directors of the companies involved urging shareholders to support or reject. But it would still be a little surprising, at least, to see directors of a bidding company in open opposition to one another. In 1972 it was not far short of scandalous. The City did not work that way. Inchcape's motives were impugned; so were the motives of Lord Poole, for Lazard's began the deal by working for both parties.

Geddes, just back from holiday, called an emergency board meeting for 29 August – although it was a bank holiday and no P&O Board had ever met on such a day before. Inchcape was there; Poole was not. Nothing was accomplished beyond vigorous disagreement. The following day, Poole returned. The Board met again, and with the exception of Inchcape, agreed with Geddes and Poole. There the matter could have ended – if Geddes had been able to have formal offer documents ready to sign. But, with group figures scattered all over the world, formal documents could not be prepared until 14 September; and the day before they were ready, another merchant bank, Morgan Grenfell, announced that with major P&O shareholders, it was going to examine the proposals.

Doubts were fanned into a renewed blaze: either Morgan Grenfell was working for a third party, probably to bid for P&O, or else – as it truthfully said – the bank was working on its own behalf, in which case it was questioning the accuracy of the merchant banks already involved. Either way it was a startling development, and at the P&O board meeting of 14 September, two executive directors decided to oppose the bid. The immediate effect was for the Stock Exchange temporarily to suspend dealings in P&O shares. Five days later, the company held a disastrous press conference, when their senior banking adviser maintained it was impossible to put a value on their ships effectively overturning decades of company accounting in which physical assets gave shares their real value. Another director publicly turned against the Bovis deal. Stating that information about profits and assets was inadequate, Morgan Grenfell submitted a 15-point questionnaire to Geddes. His answers were clear on Bovis, vague on P&O; and then the existence of another possible bidder was announced. Once again, shares were temporarily suspended; this time there really was another bidder. It was Lord Inchcape. As Chairman of the Inchcape group of companies, he offered to buy P&O for £230 million – almost 2½ times the value given the group under the Bovis arrangement.

In less than a week P&O's shares went up by more than 10 per cent. Since the original announcement, the *Financial Times* (FT) shipping index had risen by 10 per cent as well. But there seemed no end to the shocks in the City, for now Bovis offered new terms to P&O – terms which increased P&O's share of the proposed group from 59½ per cent to 63½ per cent. A biddee company was not meant to try and reduce its stake like that. It suggested that the original agreement had seriously undervalued P&O, as the dissidents claimed. And, after rising steadily for over two years, the FT's building and construction index had fallen by 10 per cent. An extraordinary general meeting of P&O shareholders, scheduled for 12 October, was adjourned to Thursday, 9 November. More than ever, it appeared that P&O would be Bovis's saviour, not the other way around; and on 9 November P&O's past Chairman Sir Donald Anderson published his considered opposition to any deal. That day's extraordinary general meeting, adjourned from 12 October, altered the company's voting structure in favour of institutional shareholders. Hitherto, every £100 of stock was allowed one vote, with a maximum of 20 votes per stockholder. Now the basis became one share, one vote; and on Friday 17 November the final extraordinary general meeting was due. A proxy race began.

The weekend brought one final intervention: Sir Donald revealed that if both the Bovis and Inchcape bids were rejected, Lord Inchcape was prepared to become P&O Chairman if asked. The group could revert to the *status quo*, with an Inchcape at its head. Involving two of the most prestigious names in the company's history, it was a powerful proposal; and particularly so, because the two names were joined. Historically, the Anderson/Orient Line side of P&O and the Inchcape/British India side had been, if not opponents, at least acknowledged rivals. For the two camps to unite thus in public opposition to the bid showed how strongly they both disliked it. Yet it seemed the names might have lost their charisma: by Tuesday, 14 November, 14 million votes had been counted, and they were running 2:1 in favour of the Bovis deal.

But Morgan Grenfell held a further 10 million proxies. Just before 3 p.m. on Wednesday, 15 November, the voting deadline, they were given in. They were counted next morning, and suddenly Geddes and Sanderson knew they would lose. Institutional votes were equally divided – but the small shareholders were united against Bovis, and turned a 2:1 acceptance into a 5:2 rejection.

Nearly 60 years before, after negotiating the amalgamation of P&O and B I in utter secrecy, Sir Thomas Sutherland and the first Lord Inchcape had been able to present a *fait accompli* with scarcely a protest. At the extraordinary general meeting on 17 November 1972 the shareholders' rebellion against their Chairman was all too clear: when Geddes acknowledged his plans had been defeated, cheers burst out. When he said he would resign, there was loud applause. When a call

Kenneth James William
Mackay, Third Earl of
Inchcape, P&O Chairman
1973–83 and now the
company's President.
(Oil by Douglas Anderson,
1983)

came from the floor for Lord Poole to resign as well, hisses greeted his name; and when Poole said he would resign and that Lazard's would waive its fee, he was jeered. Times had changed indeed.

It was a miserable period for the company. No one, once the blood had been let, could deny a feeling of compassion for Ford Geddes. It was sad that his long and loyal career ended in ignominious resignation. But it was done, and the group had to continue.

Executive leadership was vested in the revived post of Managing Director. As executive director of the Bulk Shipping Division under Geddes, Alexander (Sandy) Marshall had been the leading executive dissentient in the Bovis affair. On 20 November 1972 he became Managing Director; and on 10 January 1973, the third Lord Inchcape became Chairman of P&O. Unlike his grandfather, he was non-executive. Inchcape saw his own main function as 'affording guidance and counsel to the Managing Director, and assisting on major issues

affecting the group'. At least as importantly for the ordinary shareholders and the general public, though, he was also the group's figurehead.
In his first annual statement, delivered on 14 March 1973, he said
plainly, 'It is now clear that the merger with Bovis . . . would have been a
mistake'; and he was able to show why. Profits for the first six months of
1972 – the depressing picture which had led Geddes towards Bovis –
had been only £830,000. But for the financial year as a whole, P&O's
group pre-tax profit was £12.3 million.

The watchword now was flexibility. P&O would remain a shipping
company, as always, but any profitable interest could become part of the
group, without prejudice – and any unprofitable interest would be
altered or dropped swiftly, without sentiment. Within P&O itself,
passenger operations were rearranged into regional cruising areas –
Europe, West Coast North America, and Australasia – and, although
passengers were still conveyed from A to B when moving ships from one
cruising base to another, line voyages ended as air fares became cheaper.
To underline the change, a leading US cruise operator, Princess
Cruises, was purchased in 1974. Ranger Fishing was losing several
hundred thousand pounds a year, and was sold; simultaneously,
interests were bought in existing oil- and gas-producing fields in the
United States. But the really surprising acquisition of the new Inchcape
regime was Bovis.

After the turmoil between them, it was the last company an outsider
would have imagined as a member of the P&O group. However, after
gaining a stake in Bovis, there had been no particular reason to dispose
of it. It was not the idea which had been wrong – shipping cycles and
construction cycles could smooth each other out. It was simply the
figures which had been wrong. When P&O bought the rest of the
company in 1974, there was no hesitation, for the price was a fifth of the
amount of the 1972 proposals.

The new company had scarcely been absorbed into the group before a

P&O's takeover of Princess
Cruises gave it a vastly
improved foothold on the US
West Coast. The Los
Angeles company celebrated
its tenth birthday not long
afterwards, and this cartoon
depicts P&O Cruises' Harry
Spanton presenting
Princess's founder Stan
McDonald with new ships to
enlarge his fleet.
(Cartoon by Manning, 1975)

far greater change was imposed from outside. In 1974, OPEC quadrupled the price of oil, bringing steep inflation and financial chaos to the entire industrialized world. In that year P&O achieved an outstanding new level of profitability, with pre-tax profits of £48.5 million. However, Inchcape warned that part of this was artificial, attributable to inflation, and that figures for 1975 would be lower: 'The slackening in world economies has taken some time to affect shipping.' He was right: 1975 produced less than half the profit of 1974 – only £22.7 million. And because the group financial year was altered to coincide with the calendar year, that much lower figure represented 15 months' trading. Moreover, the property market in Europe and Canada declined suddenly and sharply. Yet the Chairman was not dismayed; the 1974–5 financial period included two fourth quarters, which usually had the worst results of any year. And P&O was now a very diverse group. It sailed ships. It also produced oil and gas in 'a modest but growing' manner. And, through Bovis, 'we construct hospitals, roads, houses'. With such varied international interests, 'we can therefore look to the future with confidence'.

The new year, 1976, brought pride to the Chairman: at the end of May he was elected President of the General Council of British Shipping, an annual post which his grandfather had held three times. It brought excitement to the company as well, for at last North Sea oil was discovered in what was later named the Beatrice field, in which P&O held a 15 per cent stake. But the confusion created by OPEC's decision was far from over. With the late 1960s remembered for their strikes, the late 1970s were embittered by runaway inflation hitting 26 per cent, and by national financial crisis as sterling collapsed in the autumn of 1976. High base rates of bank lending meant an increase that year of £14 million in property borrowing alone, with £50 million added in overseas borrowings; inflation meant that an apparent slight rise in pre-tax profits to £31.1 million was largely illusory.

Retrenchment and redeployment was the order of the day. The group's tanker investment had already peaked with four 215,000-ton vessels delivered in 1969–70, and one ship of 275,000 tons completed in 1974. Perhaps fortunately, a 414,000-ton tanker ordered in the mid-1970s was renegotiated first as two bulk carriers, and ultimately as two cargo ships and two ferries. Part of the equity of P&O Australia Ltd was issued to the Australian public, and the issue was well subscribed. P&O's ship repair companies were sold to British Shipbuilders. Ships themselves were sold and new deliveries postponed. Staff numbers were reduced. Construction, road haulage, freight forwarding and energy (oil and gas) gave the group 'a measure of strength and stability'; yet though the house flag now flew over oil fields in a dozen states of the USA, in the UK applications for authority to develop the Beatrice field met with delay after delay. And in spite of every effort, profits for 1978 plummetted to £18.4 million.

Coming on top of everything else, it was one of the most serious declines the company had faced in over 140 years. Even Inchcape believed that 'P&O's own future might be at risk'; and in emergency, the company turned to him. In September 1978 he became Chief

Executive in addition to his post as Chairman. Two further Managing Directors were appointed: Oliver Brooks and Richard Adams, former chairman of BI, who replaced Lord Inchcape as Chief Executive in 1981. Drastic reorganization began. As Lord Inchcape reminded the shareholders, 'A business must be able to contract as well as expand, and to change its shape in a changing world.' The fleets of the General Cargo and Bulk Shipping divisions were reduced; commitment to 'our new and expensive' liquid petroleum gas carriers was cut; the company's interest in the Beatrice field was sold, as were the group's American oil- and gas-production interests; the entire Energy Division, 'established with high hopes', was disbanded; and even the annual report was printed on cheaper paper than usual.

At the company's annual general meeting on 6 June 1980 Lord Inchcape noted that since the OPEC decision of 1974, P&O's fleet was numerically cut exactly in half – from 178 to 89 ships. The change was so marked that he felt obliged to explain that only about half the difference came from sales of offshore service operations, and reductions in crude oil tanker investment and dry bulk shipping. The other half came through improved technology, and he cited as an example the group's ferries to Orkney and Shetland. In 1974, six ships had carried 89,000

(*Above*)
Strathcarron (10,031 dwt) is seen here in the late 1970s livery of P&O Strath Services (formerly the General Cargo Division), but started life in 1969 as BI's *Amra*. She was equipped with a 300-ton Stulcken derrick to enable her to carry heavy or large deck cargoes such as these barges bound for the Gulf.

(*Opposite*)
The 264,591 dwt ore/oil carrier *Lauderdale*, built in 1972, was the largest ship yet built for P&O. Here she loads at the Iranian oil terminal at Kharg Island in October 1973.

Conversion of P&O Ferries'
Orkney and Shetland routes
to roll-on/roll-off ships
began in 1975 when the
1,344-grt *St Ola* went into
service between Scrabster
and Stromness. By the end of
the decade all the Group's
conventional ferries and
short-sea cargo ships had
been replaced by ro-ro
vessels.

Sir Andrew Crichton, first
Chairman of Overseas
Containers Ltd, into which
P&O's many general cargo
trades were progressively
transferred.

passengers and 101,000 tons of freight; in 1979, four ships were able to carry over 130,000 passengers and 180,000 tons of freight.

For those shareholders 'who have invested in what they have seen as predominantly a shipping company' it must have been unsettling when he remarked that there were more and more sectors of deep-sea shipping which could not be operated profitably by P&O. It can scarcely have been reassuring when he added, 'We will certainly remain in some areas of shipping.' But in fact, though P&O as a shipping company had altered its types of ships and reduced their numbers, between 1970 and 1981 its shipping tonnage had been cut by only 4 per cent, from 2.55 million to 2.45 million grt. In the public view, P&O's cruise ships were its most striking vessels; financially, however, the jewel in its shipping crown was OCL; and much of the credit for that was due to its first Chairman, Sir Andrew Crichton. From its inception in 1965 until 1973, he had shaped the company. Now, in 1981, he was about to retire from the Board of P&O, after 50 years in the group; and in 1980, P&O had increased its holding in OCL from 30.9 per cent to 44.21 per cent. Sir Andrew could retire with considerable, and justifiable, pride in his achievement.

The corrosive inflation of the 1970s was halted by a strong-willed Government restricting the money supply through high interest rates. Despite this handicap to every industry, no one in P&O would deny that the company's harsh cuts and reorganization had worked. P&O had not only averted the possibility of real disaster, but was beginning to prosper once more. The dividend for 1981 was 10 per cent; pre-tax profit was £41 million. And events of 1982 brought vessels of The Peninsular and Oriental Steam Navigation Company to a prominence which made even the least shipping-minded of investors proud of their company.

Nobody expected another local war. Hiroshima, NATO and the Cold War had taught people to think that if ever Great Britain fought again, it would be as part of a brief intercontinental nuclear conflict of superpowers. Yet on Friday, 2 April 1982, Argentinian forces invaded the Falkland Islands. In Britain, disbelief in most people swiftly gave way to confused indignation, but already Government, the armed forces, the Royal Fleet Auxiliary and the Merchant Navy were moving. Official consultations with P&O Cruises began on Friday afternoon and with P&O European Transport Services on Saturday. Late on Sunday evening the Queen signed the Order in Council enabling the Government to requisition all necessary ships. On Monday, P&O's roll-on/roll-off freight ferry *Elk* and the great cruise ship *Canberra* were ordered to Southampton to be under Royal Navy control.

It was over 40 years since the company's last experience of requisitioning but the system still worked smoothly. Within hours of receiving her orders, *Elk* had left her usual route between Middlesbrough and Gothenburg, and on Tuesday she was in Southampton loading ammunition and light tanks. On Wednesday, *Canberra* arrived back from a three-month world cruise, and as her passengers disembarked at 9 a.m., naval and military personnel were ready to begin her conversion to a helicopter-carrying troopship. The following day 3,000 men of 40 and 42 Commando, Royal Marines, and 3 Para – 3rd Battalion the Parachute Regiment – began embarking, and on 9 April, one week after the Argentinian invasion, both *Elk* and *Canberra* set sail for war. It was Good Friday.

Altogether, six vessels from P&O and its associated companies joined the contingent of ships taken up from trade – STUFT, to use the ungainly acronym – which contributed to Operation Corporate, the official name of the Falklands conflict. As well as *Elk* and *Canberra*, the large North Sea ferry *Norland*, the 50-per cent-owned tanker *Anco Charger* and the cargo liner *Strathewe* were all taken up. And so was *Uganda*, the famous, favourite educational cruise ship, requisitioned from Alexandria with 70 teachers, 245 independent passengers and 944 schoolchildren on board.

P&O ships made up 10 per cent of the STUFT group, and it was not only company vessels which went south. Some 860 P&O personnel remained with their ships. It would be invidious to select names - some were old enough to remember World War II, many were too young to have ever seen combat at first hand, but all, from captains to stewardesses, were very brave. For when they set sail they did not know what would happen, when they would return, or even if they would return.

In 65 hours, between Friday, 16 April and Monday, 19 April, *Uganda*

Uganda, (16,907 grt), built in 1952 for BI's East Africa run but an educational cruise ship since 1968, was requisitioned for the Falklands campaign and converted to a hospital ship at Gibraltar.

was converted in the dockyard at Gibraltar to her new role as a hospital ship. *Elk* and *Canberra* arrived at Ascension on 20 April, when *Elk* was provided with a helicopter flight deck to augment those in *Canberra*. Six days later *Norland* left Portsmouth with 2 Para on board. On the 28th, *Uganda* reached Ascension, and as diplomacy faltered, a 200-mile Total Exclusion Zone was declared around the Falklands. But the threat of force did not deter either side, and when the Argentinian cruiser *General Belgrano* was torpedoed on 2 May and the British destroyer *HMS Sheffield* was bombed, conflict became a savage reality.

On 11 May *Uganda* reached her station in the South Atlantic. Within a day her first casualties, survivors of *HMS Sheffield*, were embarked for treatment. On 13 May came a sombre prediction that her work would not stop there, for on that day the decision was made to land troops on the islands. In preparation for the landings, 40 Commando was transferred by landing craft from *Canberra* to *HMS Fearless* and 3 Para to *HMS Intrepid*. It was 19 May – *Canberra*'s 21st birthday.

The assault force entered Falkland Sound during the night of 20–21 May, heading for San Carlos Water, the landing ground selected from charts for its apparent good natural defences against air attack. *Norland* was the first ship to enter San Carlos. With her, in addition to Royal Navy vessels, were *Canberra* and a Townsend Thoresen ship, *Europic*

(*Above*)
P&O's 12,988-grt North Sea passenger/cargo ferry *Norland* and *HMS Intrepid* under Argentine bombardment in San Carlos Water on 24 May 1982, three days after the merchant ship had discarged men of 2 Para into landing craft for the first British assault.
(Oil by David Cobb, 1983)

(*Left*)
Bridge personnel of the 8,593-dwt *Elk* take appropriate precautions during an Air Raid Warning Red on one of her five runs into San Carlos with vehicles and ammunition. Though fitted with two anti-aircraft guns, she never actually fired a shot in anger.

Canberra, 'The Great White Whale', was given an unprecedented reception when she returned to Southampton on 11 July 1982, undamaged after her service as the main troopship in the Falklands campaign.

Ferry. And shortly after dawn, the Argentinian air force was overhead.

Whatever preconceptions the British public had about Argentinian pilots, they rapidly proved themselves to be a well-trained and thoroughly professional air force. It was only because they chose naval targets that the merchant ships in San Carlos escaped unharmed. All were still in their civilian colours – *Norland* black and white, *Canberra* all white, *Europic Ferry* bright red: each a distinctly visible sitting target. Cunard's container ship *Atlantic Conveyor*, with a radar profile very like an aircraft carrier, was destroyed later, at sea; but P&O was fortunate. No company personnel were killed, nor was any company ship structurally damaged at all.

From the first landings to the ceasefire on 14 June and beyond, the P&O ships participated fully, replenishing stores, weapons and ammunition, taking men ashore, receiving and treating the wounded, burying the dead. Long before the end, they had acquired affectionate nicknames – *Elk*, with her cargo of weaponry, became the *Toybox*, and later *Elk Royal*. From the popular television series MASH, *Uganda* became NOSH – Naval Ocean-going Surgical Hospital. *Mother Hen* was another nickname for her, since she coordinated the movements of *Hecla*, *Herald* and *Hydra*, her chicks – three Royal Naval survey ships

198

converted to ambulance carriers – as well as the Argentine hospital ships. But inevitably, the most famous P&O ship down there was *Canberra*, and equally inevitably, she became the *Great White Whale*.

Following the Argentinian surrender, *Canberra* and *Norland* took over 6,000 prisoners of war back to South America, and after 94 days away, *Canberra* returned to Southampton in triumph on Sunday, 11 July. The warmth of her welcome back was overwhelming – an estimated 30,000 people came to celebrate; hundreds of vessels from dinghies and yachts to tugs and the P&O ferry *Dragon* escorted her in; media enthusiasm made it a national and international event. Every task-force ship, whether Royal Navy or Merchant Navy, met a similar reception. Every merchant ship came in garlanded with streamers and impromptu banners; one of the best of those was hung on *Uganda*. Her medical team, which included P&O personnel, had treated 730 'in-patients', including 150 Argentinians, and had performed 504 operations. Returning in the *Mother Hen* were members of 16 Field Ambulance, RAMC, the only Royal Army Medical Unit ashore during the campaign; and over her side they hung a banner saying: 'We came – we saw – we treated.'

14

A NEW ERA

The emergence of new leadership, the passing of control from one dynasty to another in a great commercial enterprise has frequently involved change. Less often has the process turned on the very existence of the business, but so it was with P&O. A stage was reached when extinction of the independent company was at hand. For this reason, the developments, actions and consequences attending the traumatic crisis attained a level akin to high drama.

The story must claim a prominent place in a book which might not have been written if the results had been otherwise, or at best, would be a record only of the past.

The germ of the change to come lay in Lord Inchcape's wise decision, in 1979, to seek two or three new and younger directors. In the face of the altering spread and character of the company's operations, which he was anxious to progress, he was concerned to strengthen the Board with members whose experience lay in fields beyond shipping. Accordingly, he asked the non-executive directors to keep a look-out for suitable candidates.

Two able directors were found, Peter Cazalet and Gurth Hoyer Millar. The former had, in fact, a close shipping connection since he was responsible for British Petroleum's large tanker fleet. Hoyer Millar came from the great Sainsbury supermarket chain. However, Lord Inchcape still felt that a director or two should be sought who were younger than these recent appointees and with specific financial experience.

This further request produced no result and Sir Andrew Crichton decided to put forward the name of Jeffrey Sterling for consideration. Crichton, as Chairman of Overseas Containers, had got to know Sterling when negotiating with him for the purchase of Beagle House, Aldgate, as a new headquarters for OCL. He was impressed by him personally and by his experience and impressive achievements in the property world. Sterling was, at that time, deeply immersed in the last stages of the arduous task of salvaging the wreck of Town & City Properties, a major property business which almost went under in the crash of 1974. He had been called in by a number of leading institutions headed by Prudential Assurance and Barclays Bank who were heavily involved with very considerable loans at stake. Sterling's skill and gift for inspiring a team, with his principal colleague Bruce MacPhail, in the long years of anxiety and concentrated effort, saved the day and earned the undoubted gratitude and respect of those who had placed their faith in him. His reputation in the City stood high.

During informal conversations, Crichton had noted Sterling's lively and intelligent interest in the new system of containerisation that was about to sweep the shipping industry. Clearly, he was fascinated by the economics of the revolution in transport.

Crichton then told Sterling that he wished to suggest his candidature for membership of the P&O Board and Sterling agreed to see Lord Inchcape.

Crichton explained Sterling's background to Lord Inchcape emphasizing that the former was not, in fact, primarily a property man and that his basic training and experience had been in financial affairs; his start was on the Stock Exchange in London followed by spells in other international markets before founding his own financial group, Sterling Guarantee Trust, in 1969. A discussion was arranged with Lord Inchcape who took a favourable view and interviews followed with two senior P&O directors, Sir Eric Drake (ex-Chairman of British Petroleum) and Ian Denholm of the great Glasgow ship management firm. Both gave emphatic approval and Sterling joined the P&O Board in February 1980.

In the spring of that year the first flutterings of the breeze which was to develop into a storm could be felt. Furness Withy, after clearance from the Monopolies and Mergers Commission, had been taken over by the CY Tung shipping empire in Hong Kong, and comment was growing on the possibility of other Hong Kong shipowners amply provided with cash casting eyes on major British shipping groups, which could only mean P&O and Ocean Transport. But it was not until November 1981 that the wind of speculation began to blow more strongly with an unexplained and persistent rise in the price of P&O stock. Rumours swirled and eventually crystallized in the conviction that the activities stemmed from the intentions of Carrian Investments, an aggressive if somewhat mysterious group in Hong Kong, whose market capitalization had grown from £22 million to £44 million in two years and included a substantial fleet of ships. This was characteristic of the then heady, euphoric scene in Hong Kong but indicated the underlying capacity of some Chinese millionaires to pay for an acquisition of this size out of the small change in their pockets. By December 1981, the Carrian group was in trouble and the squall died down as quickly as it had sprung up, but the warning was there: it was that P&O was vulnerable.

The next stage in the saga was the Annual General Meeting in June 1982, when Lord Inchcape stated his intention of giving up the Chairmanship at the following AGM in 1983, when he would have passed 65, the retiring age for an executive director. He indicated that his successor would be Ian Denholm, then his deputy, and that he himself would be willing to continue as non-executive Deputy Chairman. He added that Rodney Leach and Derek Hall would support Denholm as Managing Directors. Subsequently, this early commitment, so far in advance of the handover of the Chairmanship, was considered to have been a little injudicious.

Two senior men occupying key posts – Oliver Brooks, Finance Director, and Dick Adams, long-serving Managing Director – were also due to retire. This knowledge, in an atmosphere of vulnerability, was interpreted as a possible weakening of the top managerial structure.

Be that as it may, within a very short time a bid for P&O was made by Trafalgar House, owners of Cunard. Trafalgar's Chairman, Nigel Broackes (later Sir Nigel) dominated the group, which had expanded dramatically under his leadership in property, construction and shipping. Coincidentally, he was a contemporary of Sterling and had advanced in the world of business by much the same hard road of experience and ambition. He was shrewd and adept to a degree in the art of the takeover.

It was clear that P&O was faced with a truly serious contender. Broackes launched his campaign with a lordly tone of co-operation and on the theme of the synergy of the two groups. But his purpose was deadly.

Sir Jeffrey Sterling, CBE, Chairman of P&O since 1983.

The Trafalgar terms were considered unacceptable and not in the interests of stockholders. Lord Inchcape promptly withdrew his proposal for retirement and the connected changes in the Board. He declared he would conduct the defence and see it through. At the AGM on the 9 June 1983 Lord Inchcape gave a spirited rejoinder and made the Board's total opposition clear.

A point of acute danger and anxiety had arrived; so had Nemesis.

It was soon apparent that the issue would rest with the institutions with large shareholdings. In the last analysis they would be influenced by their decision as to which group would prove the more valuable investment. P&O was in an awkward and uncomfortable spot. Endeavours to change the direction of effort into more profitable channels could not be brought to fruition in the near term. The balance sheet and cash resources needed instant attention.

To have some flexibility to marshal and present their forces, time was essential; it was of the essence.

In view of Cunard's interest in shipping, there was a good case for referring the bid to the Monopolies and Mergers Commission. Happily, this was achieved and gave a breathing space of up to ten months or so, but as it was becoming increasingly apparent that the problem was primarily financial, it was urgent that someone equipped to deal with the situation be found.

Crichton had earlier urged Lord Inchcape that the appointment of Sterling as a Deputy Chairman would have shown a red light to predators, especially since he and Broackes were business friends and Broackes knew Sterling's mind and methods. The reverse was also the case. After the bid the need for decision was again pressed, with the added reminder of Sterling's influence and standing with the City generally and the institutions in particular, several of them being grateful for his successful efforts on their behalf over the rehabilitation of Town & City Properties.

Lord Inchcape delayed and said he was inclined to seek a candidate from outside the company with the reversion of succeeding to the chair in due course. He then decided to enquire whether the Bank of England could produce a candidate from the records they kept of leading figures in industry and finance.

He was met with a prompt and brief reply: 'how much further do you have to look than a member of your own Board – Mr Jeffrey Sterling'. Lord Inchcape was convinced and Sterling became Deputy Chairman on 6 July 1983 succeeding him as Chairman on 1 November 1983. Lord Inchcape became President of P&O.

Sterling flung himself into the task of dealing with the immediate financial situation, achieving swift and effective sales and the elimination of certain American ventures which although profitable, were attended by potentially dangerous contingent liabilities which he was not prepared to risk. It was not known when the Commission would give its verdict but Sterling was determined to anticipate it, whichever way it might go, by producing the balance sheet and accounts for 1983 two months ahead of the usual date of publication. This deliberate and remarkable 'forced march' involved monumental efforts by the whole

Among the many former Sterling Guarantee Trust activities now part of P&O is the ownership and management of the Earl's Court and Olympia exhibition centres in London. The International Boat Show at Olympia is one of their best-known exhibitions.

organization and was received literally with a gasp of admiration and astonishment by the financial world. His appointment as Chairman had signalled a fundamental change in the Company's position and this further example of his energy and skill had a major impact on the confidence and attitudes of those investors and institutions where decisions would determine P&O's independence.

Early in 1984, the Monopolies Commission gave its consent to Trafalgar House proceeding with its bid. Sterling claimed this was immaterial to the outcome of the fight; P&O was now ready and able to stand on its own feet. The final and conclusive stamp set on Sterling's intensive efforts was the simple endorsement of this view by Trafalgar House. Their bid was withdrawn. Broackes retreated from the field of battle and not ungraciously.

The victory had, without question, saved P&O from what would have been extinction as a company, and the credit went unreservedly to Sterling. A new era had opened, and it was clear that what had not been achieved had now to be undertaken and within an adequate and acceptable time scale. Forthwith, Sterling dealt with some of the weaker managerial situations in the divisions and addressed the managers of P&O. His message was direct and powerful: he was 'profoundly conscious' that his position as Chairman came as a privilege, not as a right; and by the same token 'our financial success and personal welfare depend upon our ability to produce a level of profit in each of our businesses that justified our claim to that title of "manager". In the absence of that constantly improving financial result, we have no claim – historical or otherwise.'

This theme of individual responsibility, to which he later linked reward, was an essential part of his commercial philosophy and one which he developed again when the time came for the merging of Sterling Guarantee Trust into the new, fully fledged P&O Group.

He also took an early opportunity to become chairman of Overseas Containers Holdings (OCH), in effect the partnership of the owners controlling OCL. As P&O held the largest share ($47\frac{1}{2}$ per cent) in this consortium, he was fully justified and well advised to do so. From the time of his joining the Board, he had realized the great importance of this investment, representing as it did the whole residue of P&O's general cargo-carrying capacity world wide.

Sir Jeffrey was knighted in the New Year's Honours List for 1985.

Shortly afterwards, plans were announced for a merger between P&O and Sterling Guarantee Trust. It did not come as a surprise; the idea of a get-together had looked increasingly probable. Indeed, it had clearly been an objective Sterling had foreseen and hoped to achieve.

Sterling Guarantee Trust (SGT) incorporated the once again rich and profitable Town & City Properties, which Sterling and MacPhail had raised from near ruin, but also included in its activities Butters Warehousing, industrial tools (Buck & Hickman), catering (Sutcliffes), a security organization and the ownership and management of exhibition centres at Earls Court and Olympia. All were basically service industries which had provided much needed sustenance during the long haul in bringing Town & City back to health.

SGT was the essential core of Sterling's career. It was in the process of its foundation and growth that he emerged for what he was – a highly successful entrepreneur with acute financial judgment both in the selection of businesses and of men to run them. He displayed an outstanding gift for what can best be described as controlled delegation, the lack of which has so often brought other energetic aspirants to grief. In the building up of SGT, Sterling would be the first to assert the immense contribution made by his principal collaborator and support, Bruce MacPhail, whose strength lay in his exceptional brilliance as an administrator.

As mentioned earlier, Sterling was never primarily a property man and there is little doubt that his financial and service business experience was fundamental to his understanding and development of the two divisions of SGT – real estate and services. By the time of the merger these had combined in a group comparable to P&O in its content and quality, amply justifying such a step.

Though there had been doubts in some quarters as to the relevance of

the merger with P&O, it was soon recognized that the injection was of the first importance to P&O in terms of assets, cash and profits. That it was truly complementary was soon appreciated and it only needed the stimulation of rationalization and management to bring it to fruition. As Sir Jeffrey Sterling said, 'Welded together they have an exciting future.'

One result of the merger was to produce a group with a capitalization of £1,000 million.

The first Annual General Meeting of the newly born group was a momentous occasion and took place on 22 April 1985. It was followed the same evening by a dinner which Sterling gave exclusively for managers from both sides of the previously separate companies. His theme, once more, was that responsibility lay with managers given much scope, linked with rewards attending their results. It was an inspired move to let new colleagues see each other and hear his policy.

After the formalities of merging had been sealed, much of the year 1985 was devoted to knitting together the component parts to ensure the maximum benefit for the newly combined Group. This was no mean task of administration and concentrated largely on redeploying resources both in terms of men and material assets involved in the service industries of the two sides. The careful choice of managers to rationalize operations and to control and assess investment was a basic requirement. Encouraging and effective co-operation resulted.

The extensive P&O road haulage fleets linked with ferry services and the country-wide warehousing facilities of SGT formed a significant chain of through transport, all against the background of the prevailing and almost universal method of packing and carriage in containers.

The major investment in passenger ships engaged exclusively in the cruising business presented a problem on its own. Due to the extremely competitive state of the market, it was a cause for anxiety and was failing to yield an adequate return on the very large capital involved.

(Opposite)
A model of Chelsea Harbour on the Thames in London, a P&O and Globe Investment Trust PLC development. The project managers are Town & City Properties and the construction managers are Bovis Construction Ltd.

A Ferrymasters tractor and trailer disembark from P&O's cargo ferry *Norsea* at Ipswich after crossing on the North Sea Ferries service from Rotterdam. P&O European Transport Services' road haulage fleet specializes, among its other activities, in through-transport operations linked to dedicated cargo ferry services.

P&O's head office had for nearly 150 years been in or near the traditional centre of British shipping, Leadenhall Street in the City of London. Symbolic of change in the nature of the Group and his own management style, Sir Jeffrey Sterling moved the head office to new surroundings, 79 Pall Mall in the West End of London.

Rationalization and reductions in operating costs were urgent and these problems called for attention and action which continued into 1986.

Extensive reorganisation of staff and premises was also carried out. This aimed at implementing the Chairman's views on the part that sensible decentralization could play in giving managers an added sense of independence in recognizing their responsibilities, and in achieving their own personal results.

The few survivors who had worked in the old P&O Building in Leadenhall Street, the original freehold, on the site of a coaching inn complete with courtyard, and with its own water supply from an underground spring, known throughout the shipping fraternity simply as No. 122, had seen it demolished in 1964. During rebuilding P&O had moved to a complex of offices centred on Beaufort House in Gravel Lane off Houndsditch, known to P&O officers afloat irreverently as 'Grovel Lane' when they reported there. The fine new building was occupied in 1969, some of it being let at remunerative rates, but later gradually vacated. It was sold by Sterling in June 1984 for the considerable and welcome sum of £71 million, as part of his actions in adjusting capital and balance sheet positions.

The same year Sterling took the dramatic step of moving the head office of P&O from the hallowed ground of the shipping industry in the heart of the City of London, to 79 Pall Mall close to his former SGT premises in Carlton Gardens. This address, renamed Peninsular House, was on the site of the residence occupied by Nell Gwyn, the favourite mistress of Charles II.

He chose headquarters so situated because his style of management meant that he did not want to be surrounded, as were his predecessors, by the whole machinery, nuts and bolts of shipowning and day-to-day management. He wished to be at the centre of the empire, yet separated from it, together with his closest confidants and support staff, free to survey and control the scene objectively. The personnel in 79 Pall Mall was reduced to 24 with a finance department numbering 32 next door in Schomberg House. The staff of the City HQ had numbered some 600 at its peak in the early 1970s.

The year 1985 produced record profits for P&O totalling £125 million, the largest in the company's history. These results, published early in April 1986, confirmed confidence in the whole venture and standing of the enlarged group.

Following this boost, and prior to the Annual General Meeting on 28 April, two events of magnitude took place. Sterling launched a double-headed bid of vital strategic importance in terms of reinforcing the shipping and property sectors of the P&O Group.

First was the purchase of the remaining 53 per cent of OCL held by Ocean Transport & Trading and British & Commonwealth Shipping, making P&O sole owner of the container shipping consortium and OCL a full subsidiary. This was accomplished with the ready agreement of the two vendors. At the time of this move only three of the original four partners remained. P&O, the major shareholders, had long considered the desirability of full control. One of the alternatives open was to bid outright for OTT, old rivals of P&O in the Far East trades as Holt's Blue Funnel Line. Sensing this option, Sterling, shrewdly, had early on bought 3 per cent of Ocean for SGT at what proved to be a very modest price. As Chairman of P&O he raised the stake to 13 per cent, thus enhancing his influence in OCL's affairs. Consequently, it was widely felt that the day would come when Ocean would be taken over. However, the latter was changing its character and was backing away from shipping, aiming at development on different lines. Accordingly, it welcomed the arrangement to sell its OCL share provided that the threat of a potential bid for the entire business was lifted by P&O agreeing to sell its existing 13 per cent. This P&O did by placing the OTT shares with institutions in the market. It was also part of the bargain that P&O's 50 per cent interest in Panocean Storage & Transport should be sold to OTT. These disposals significantly reduced the cost to P&O of acquiring OCL. The Cayzers of British & Commonwealth had, to all intents, withdrawn from shipping and willingly sold, accepting P&O shares as part of their deal.

In advising stockholders of the acquisition of OCL the Chairman stated it was in accordance with P&O's policy of expanding its major activities and concentrating management effort in certain clearly defined sectors. He added that it also extended further P&O's aim of developing its interests in the Far East and Australasia.

The decision to follow investment in shipping was not taken lightly, nor was it overlooked that OCL would find it difficult, in the face of increasing competition from newcomers, to maintain profits on the record scale of 1985. The view was taken, however, that Britain's first major consortium committed, exclusively, to owning a large fleet of

P&O's long-standing links with the Far East and Australasia have been rekindled by the full acquisition of Overseas Containers Ltd. *Arafura* is one of two ships of OCL subsidiary Australia Japan Container Line linking Australia with Japan as part of the company's worldwide container services.

Bovis Construction have been responsible for many impressive buildings, not least the International Conference Centre in the heart of London, opposite Westminster Abbey and within sight of the Houses of Parliament, opened in 1986.

economic container ships equipped with the ancilliary services required of through transport, and under first-class operational management, was at the right and profitable end of the shipping business, and capable of contributing to P&O's future success over the years. Unburdened by debt and with little capital expenditure in prospect, OCL could face a future in which competitors might be eroded by the old-established shipping experience of overstretched resources.

For P&O, it was something of a turn of the wheel; having been a carrier of freight since its inception, the Company emerged as the predominant British owner of cargo liners.

The second bid, the larger in financial terms at £377 million, was for the major property company Stock Conversion.

The objective was again the same – a further significant step in P&O's policy of improving the quality of earnings and developing existing business. The bid was rejected by Stock Conversion.

Sterling had always been averse to contested bids, much preferring the arranged version as better calculated to reduce risk and cost. In fact, he had his own plans to circumvent a rebuttal and would probably not have embarked on a takeover without having them in reserve.

From a partial interest P&O had acquired in European Ferries ran a stake in Stockley, a young, dynamic property firm which owned 26½ per cent of Stock Conversion, much to the latter's embarrassment. Sterling, who was close to and friendly with the owners of Stockley, obtained the irrevocable support of their share, and from that proceeded to build up further ammunition to a point when, after only six days, Stock Conversion conceded defeat and agreed a full takeover, with the value of the bid raised to £402 million.

HRH The Princess of Wales named the 44,348-grt *Royal Princess*, at the time the world's most advanced passenger ship, at Southampton in November 1984. P&O's most luxurious cruise vessel, she was designed for the lucrative North American market.

Overleaf
(*Top left*)
Formed in 1965, Bovis Homes is one of the largest private housebuilding companies in the United Kingdom, completing some 3,000 quality homes each year on a variety of projects ranging from a small rural scheme of five detached houses to a whole village for 7,000 people.

(*Centre*)
Buck & Hickman, founded in 1842, are the largest national and international distributor of engineer's tools and equipment in the UK.

(*Bottom left*)
Sutcliffe Catering Group are one of the largest staff catering management companies in the UK, with their mainstream business the provision of catering services for people at work – approaching a million meals every week.

(*Far right above*)
P&O owns and/or manages Arndale Shopping Centres throughout the UK, a total of nearly 5 million square feet. Town & City have been the largest UK developers of shopping space since the War, and founded their own security company, Sterling Guards, who have since extended their services to outside clients.
(*Far right below*) The Arndale Centre in Manchester.

The result was a substantial addition to P&O's real estate interests providing managers with a fine, mature portfolio on which to work, as well as a useful connection for Bovis Construction's activities. It could only be described as a very major coup bringing P&O into the first three most influential property, investment and development groups. It provided P&O with further ballast.

At the AGM on 28 April 1986 the Chairman was questioned on his thoughts for future acquisitions. This gave him the opportunity of making an important statement on the subject. The kernel was in his emphatic words: 'we are not in the acquisition business for the sake of it; we are not an acquisition-led company'. He clearly wished to dispel any impression that he would be party to giving priority to bidding and dealing to maintain momentum. In his view, mainstream companies must have the capability of growing organically without acquisitions, at a rate which would provide shareholders with a reasonable return. If, however, from time to time, a way was found to accelerate growth by acquisition, then it would be a logical step to take. He suggested that both the moves just made were absolutely logical extensions for two of the P&O Group's main divisions.

The middle of 1986 found P&O in the billionaire class with a strong financial base supporting a wide spread of sound operations and assets under first-class management; it was a gratifying situation towards the end of 150 years of existence.

Only time will give the necessary perspective to assess the latest years of the P&O story. Financial results and merger documents are only part of the evidence; events, decisions or personalities may be given too much weight or dismissed too lightly – judgment must be left to history. But P&O is stronger now than ever before for two reasons: its ever-present philosophy of maintaining the very highest standards of service, and the varied strands which it has woven into what was once a one-route, one-contract steamship operator. Some Group companies are older than the parent company itself, and some are very large in their own right.

One of the smallest is Anderson Hughes, shipbrokers in the City of London, named after the Orient Line Andersons, who first became involved in shipowning in 1815, at about the same time as the unrelated Arthur went to work for Brodie Willcox, and Allen Hughes, founder of Federal Steam in 1895. The development and management of the covered Arndale Shopping Centres up and down the country is by contrast a child of the 1960s.

P&O Australia is publicly quoted; it has a wide range of interests in materials handling, container terminals and stevedoring, offshore services, cold storage, and leisure – apart from deep-sea shipping, almost a microcosm of its parent, which has been represented in Australia since 1852.

Property developers Boston Wharf Company are older still, and celebrated their 150th birthday in 1986. A year earlier, Bovis had marked the centenary of the takeover by Charles W. Bovis that began

The 187,025-dwt bulk carrier *Ormond* was delivered to P&O Bulk Shipping Ltd. from the Mitsubishi yard at Nagasaki, Japan, in March 1986. She was built to carry iron ore and coal on long-term contracts.

their progression from a small building company with a reputation for quality and service to an international building and construction company with the same reputation – attributes also enjoyed by P&O's major national and international tool supplier and distributor Buck & Hickman, founded in Whitechapel in London's East End, in 1842.

P&O Bulk Shipping is a post-war enterprise as far as the gas and oil trades are concerned, but the carriage of dry bulk cargoes can be traced back to the ancestors of the Hain Steamship Company, and their origins, like P&O's, were in the 1830s. Still older, the Butlers Wharf progenitors of today's Butler's Warehousing and Distribution were already long established when Peninsular Steam vessels tied up in the Thames off the Tower, or Limehouse, or East Lane Stairs, waiting for passengers to embark in small boats.

P&O Cruises embodies the most direct line back to those original P&O passengers. There is at first glance scarcely anything comparable between a sooty paddle steamer on a voyage to the Iberian Peninsula with Her Majesty's Mails, and *Royal Princess* cruising in pristine splendour in Glacier Bay, Alaska – yet in 1836 the first *Iberia* was taking

(*Above*)
P&O Australia's widespread activities include the Australian Offshore Services fleet of vessels in support of the offshore oil and gas exploration and supply industry. Here *Lady Sally* stands by the drill ship *Regional Endeavour* flaring off BHP's Challis oil well in the Timor Sea.

(*Left*)
A giant turtle on the beach at Heron Island, one of the many attractions the rich marine life has for guests at this tropical holiday island which P&O Australia owns and runs. It is in vivid contrast to Arthur Anderson's own childhood on the beaches of Shetland in the late 18th century.

holidaymakers to Madeira, and less than a decade later P&O offered Thackeray his 'delightful Mediterranean cruise'.

The internationally famous Earls Court and Olympia exhibition centres had their beginnings in 1887 and 1886, as P&O celebrated its Golden Jubilee. A primarily twentieth-century development are the haulage concerns of P&O European Transport Services: tractor units and trailers operated by UK/Continental door-to-door operator Ferrymasters, Pandoro, their counterpart between England and Richard Bourne's Ireland and by Northern Ireland Trailers (Scotland) whose name tells you where they operate; P&O Roadways' conventional haulage; and the bulk powder and liquid tankers of P&O Roadtanks with its old-established company names, including one – Thomas Allen – with links back to James Hartley, one of the founding directors of P&O.

All the P&O European Transport Services companies proudly wear the P&O flag symbol, but the Group service that would seem most familiar to Arthur Anderson must surely be the ships of P&O Ferries linking the Scottish mainland with Orkney and his beloved Shetland, direct ancestors through the North of Scotland company of the sailing vessels that provided the first irregular service in 1890. How, one wonders, would Anderson have reacted to the huge ferries now plying the North Sea?

Far beyond the earliest plans of Willcox and Anderson, Mackinnon Mackenzie & Co provide ships' agency and related services in Pakistan and keep alive the British India connection, while P&O New Zealand carries on similar business and preserves the heritage of the New Zealand Shipping Company. Both countries are served by, and both companies serve, Overseas Containers Limited, which links the Far East, Australasia and India with Europe in much the same way as the P&O mail steamers once did, with regularity, speed, and reliability. OCL ships also ply routes to and from Africa, the Mediterranean and the Gulf, and across the Atlantic.

In Shetland, the Böd of Gremista still exists – birthplace of Arthur Anderson, joint founder of the Peninsular and Oriental Steam Navigation Company. The name Böd means fisherman's shelter; without sentiment, it is pleasant to record that, through local Shetland initiative and with help from P&O, the Böd has been restored as a museum to Anderson's memory. It is important to say without sentiment, because, if Anderson was alive today, he would not have wanted P&O – his creation – to be regarded as a thing fit only for a museum. He would have remembered the past, and treasured it, rightly. He would have been proud of the present as well; and he would probably not have been astonished at the growth or the changes. For, after a childhood spent scraping herrings on a Shetland beach, he founded a phenomenal company, one centred on trust, loyalty, efficiency, imagination, service and pride. Its focus has changed but all those qualities remain.

The Böd of Gremista, birthplace of Arthur Anderson, joint founder of P&O, still stands at Lerwick and is being restored as a museum to his memory only half a mile from where, today, his company's ferries arrive from the Scottish mainland.

Illustration Acknowledgements

The publishers are grateful to the following
for permission to reproduce their photographs:

Aldus Archive 28; *BBC Hulton Picture Library* 79, 106; *BHP Petroleum* 218 above; *Bruce Castle Museum* 32, 33, 36 below right; *Christies* 20 below, 24, 43, 45 below; *Equitable Life Assurance* and *Michael Noakes* 183; *E. T. Archive* 86; *Fine Art Society* 49; *Forbes Magazine Collection* 91 below; *Fotomas Index* 70 below; *Garrick Club* 47; *Tim Graham* 212 below; *Illustrated London News* 99 above; *Imperial War Museum* 148; *Inchcape PLC* 115; *India Office Library* 70 above; *Mansell Collection* 96, 97; *Captain J. P. Morton* 198 above; *National Army Museum* 61, 93; *National Maritime Museum* 14, 51 above, 53 below, 68 below, 69, 78, 89 below, 94, 107, 110 below, 111 below, 134 above and below; *National Portrait Gallery* 13; *Public Record Office* 19; *Quadrant Picture Library* 162; *Sydney Morning Herald* 143 above and below; *University College London* 16; *Victoria and Albert Museum* 36 above, 41; *Mr. & Mrs. R. M. Wilkinson* 127

The map on page 17 was drawn by Richard Natkiel
All other illustrations are from the P&O collection.
Picture research: Anne-Marie Ehrlich.

Index

Numbers in italics refer to illustrations